Henry's Journal
The Way It Used To Be

Best wishes and good memories,
Henry Wolff, Jr.

HENRY'S JOURNAL

The Way It Used To Be

by
Henry Wolff, Jr.

*E.I. "Sticks" Stahala
Cartoons*

Victoria Advocate Publishing Co.

Library of Congress Catalog Card Number
96-61347

ISBN 0-87244-086-9

First Edition

Copyright 1996
by
Henry Wolff, Jr.
and
The Victoria Advocate

All Rights Reserved

Victoria Advocate Publishing Co.
311 E. Constitution
Victoria, Texas 77901

Printed by

Waco, Texas

PREFACE

In two previous collections of my columns from *The Victoria Advocate*, the second oldest existing newspaper in Texas for which I have been writing "Henry's Journal" for five days a week since July of 1979, now more than 4,000 columns, I picked topics that seemed to me to be significant historically or as folklore.

This book, like *Henry's Journal Volumes I* and *II*, was put together with the same idea, although each chapter category and each selected column was picked specifically with the way it used to be as a guide. In many instances, I had dozens of columns from which to choose and had to select only those that I felt would best tell a particular story.

This book, therefore, is a series of stories from beginning to end, mostly told to me by those who remember the way it used to be.

The original date of publication is noted in parenthesis at the beginning of each individual column.

I had for some time been thinking about putting together such a compilation of columns and using illustrations from *The Advocate's* collection of "The Way It Used To Be" cartoons by the late E.I. "Sticks" Stahala, a former colleague whose appreciation for times past went back considerably farther than my own years.

The year of 1996 also seemed an appropriate year for publication of this book since it is the 150th anniversary

year of *The Victoria Advocate.*
While these stories are primarily from the newspaper's daily circulation area of some 10 counties along the mid-coastal plains of Texas, the subject matter goes well beyond the boundaries of any one area. That is the way it is with the way it used to be.

The columns appear pretty much in their original form with some modification to match style changes that I have made over the years and to correct any known errors. All are in a conversational style that I find most comfortable to write, and I hope readers of this book will find each as enjoyable as it was for me to gather and write these stories.

Of the way it used to be.

Henry Wolff, Jr.
Victoria, Texas
July 29, 1996

Contents

I	
Good Eats	1
II	
More Eats	10
III	
Sauerkraut	24
IV	
Barbers	33
V	
Home Remedies	48
VI	
School Days	64
VII	
Lye Soap	78
VIII	
Saturday Baths	88
IX	
Wash Days	91
X	
Butcher Clubs	100
XI	
Hog Killing	105
XII	
Meat Markets	112
XIII	
The Depression	119
XIV	
Home Brew	128
XV	
Muddy Roads	133

XVI
Age of the Automobile 140

XVII
Old Salty 146

XVIII
Syrup Making 153

XIX
War to End All Wars 160

XX
Old-Time Baseball 173

IN MEMORY

E.I. "Sticks" Stahala
1907 - 1984

Victoria Advocate cartoonist E.I. "Sticks" Stahala covered just about every subject concerning times past at one time or another in his Sunday cartoon series, "The Way It Used To Be," a favorite with the newspaper's readers for some 15 years before his death at the age of 77 in 1984.

For this collection of newspaper columns, all from the author's "Henry's Journal" which appears five days a week in *The Victoria Advocate*, each chapter is illustrated with one of Stahala's "The Way It Used To Be" cartoons.

This book is also dedicated in memory of Sticks Stahala and the wonderful work he did for so many years as a cartoonist and journalist.

Each cartoon originally appeared with a brief written description of the chosen subject in *The Advocate's* "Fun Magazine" until his death, at which time "Henry's Journal" was placed in the same location on the inside cover page until the magazine section was discontinued in July of 1992, so in a way it could be said some of these columns and Stahala's cartoons had already shared the same space.

The author visited with Stahala at his home in Yoakum shortly after starting "Henry's Journal," at which time he was advised to include lots of names in his column and to always make sure that each was spelled correctly.

Stahala retired in 1972 from full-time work at *The Advocate*, where he had been head of the photography department in addition to being the newspaper's cartoonist.

On a drawing table set off to one side, he could turn out a cartoon in short order and it was there where the author often watched him sketch his cartoons about the way it used to be.

He also drew other cartoons for the newspaper as well, concerning news stories and sports, and frequently illustrated a Sunday history column, "Vignettes of Old Victoria," which was written by Victoria County historian Sidney R. Weisiger.

Stahala had been drawing cartoons for *The Advocate* from the time he came to work in 1936, originally as a reporter. During the years, he had various jobs including that of managing editor.

He considered *The Advocate* his only "steady job" ever, one that lasted 36 years. Stahala continued to do his "The Way It Used To Be" weekly cartoons until his death in October of 1984.

The first of these cartoons, about two boys pumping water after school for "the widow's Jersey cow and a pre-supper reward" of home-baked pastries, appeared on July 21, 1968, with a text about "When Milk Was Just Plain Milk."

A small text always accompanied his cartoons, but for the purpose of illustrating this book only the selected cartoons are being used.

During the Great Depression, after dropping out of the University of Texas when money got tight, Stahala became an itinerant journalist and cartoonist. He worked for a number of newspapers and syndicated a cartoon series that he called "TexOddiTies," much in the style of Ripley's "Believe It or Not!"

Some of his early cartoons appear in a little book that he published in 1934. He told of peddling it during 1936 at the Texas Centennial Celebration in Dallas, shortly before he joined *The Advocate* and the year the author of "Henry's Journal" was born.

It was a good year for both.

While he had studied art in college, along with agriculture, Stahala was a natural artist.

He liked to tell about during the Depression when he traded a drawing for a meal when he was bumming around looking for work. He took a seat at a cafe counter and asked if they had any chili.

"Sure, we've got chili," the waitress replied.

"I don't see any sign," he said, and commenced to draw a picture of the waitress serving a bowl of red. He swapped it for his meal and the cafe got a sign saying it served chili.

His drawing paper was old dance placards and other advertising posters that he would collect off store windows, and there were times when he would spread an armload on the ground to make himself a spot to sleep between rides and towns when he was on the road.

"When you are young and healthy, you can do anything," he said. "That is the confidence of youth. I didn't worry about the next day. I knew I could get by."

That he did, and in the process learned a whole lot about what would in his time become the way it used to be.

One could write a book and then some about Sticks Stahala, such as why he always wore a hat inside and out, the practical jokes that he loved to pull on friends, and how he got the nickname "Sticks" along with just about every other male member of the Stahala family.

There are two versions of the "Sticks" story, one having something to do with stick candy and the other with building a fire under a stubborn donkey.

A rather modest man, E.I. "Sticks" Stahala was an enjoyable person to know, whether in person or through his cartoons.

In some small way, as illustrations in this book, hopefully his "The Way It Used To Be" cartoons will help to perpetuate the memory of one who could so wonderfully express his enjoyment of life.

With nothing more than a pencil and a piece of paper and his memories of the way it used to be, he sketched the world as he knew it.

The way it was as you will see.

I

GOOD EATS

Nowadays Hard To Find
(November 13, 1985)

It's getting harder and harder to find good eats.

I'm not talking about good food, there is lots of it around, but good eats is something entirely different that can be found only in a certain type of cafe, not a restaurant either, but a cafe. It's kind of hard to describe, but I know a good eats cafe when I see one.

You used to could find one out on the edge of almost any town, on almost any highway with more than one lane, usually near a service station or sometimes combined with such, but now most all of the original ones are gone, torn down to make room for growing city limits, or they have been turned into something else entirely, boarded up, or have simply fallen down. There were also good eats cafes in the heart of most towns, but they were a little different than the ones on the edge of town which catered more to travelers and truckers.

A good sign of a good eats cafe, in addition to a neon sign proclaiming good eats as the specialty of the house, were the number of trucks you could count out front, because that has always been the calling card of good eats. In the days when eating places were fewer and farther between it was bad news for a cafe that couldn't

attract any truckers.

Good eats didn't necessarily mean anything fancy, feel I should explain that for the younger folks who have grown up on fast food and may never have had any good eats, course some of them probably wouldn't like it much since they have never had an opportunity to develop a taste for it. Good eats had about as much to do with the style in serving as the taste of the food, and basically consisted of the same things you can get today if you look around for it — chicken fried steak, hot open beef and turkey sandwiches, chili, stew, grilled cheese sandwiches, and hamburgers with just the right amount of grease.

The best place to get good eats was at the counter, where there was generally a deputy sheriff or a constable on coffee duty, or in a booth at one of the usually oblong windows, for some reason rounded oblong picture windows and good eats cafes seem to have had something in common, course about all you could ever see out of the windows was the highway and the parking lot.

In tourist areas, it was especially nice to have a window seat because you could read the license plates while waiting on the food.

Good eats was best served with a background of honkeytonk music turned just loud enough so you couldn't hear what the people in the next booth were saying. This assured privacy and entertained at the same time, course it was never so loud you couldn't hear around your own table. Most of it was soul searching music anyway, and that's best when it is played at a volume where you can still hear the words.

I must mention the waitresses were generally bleached blondes, in their early to mid-30s, divorced, with 2.5 children — and they all knew how to say "honey" in either a husky or sorta southern voice, and the amazing thing is they didn't have to go to waitress school to learn it. It was natural, they all seemed to talk that way, and I miss that when I'm eating out. It's nice to be called honey once in awhile, but I guess women's lib probably put a stop to that. Think the last waitress that called me honey had already put in for Social Security.

Looks to me like someone could come up with a good eats franchise, could get some cooks out of the soup lines, put them through a 24-hour training school, get some part-time high school waitresses and dye their hair blonde, maybe teach them to say honey with a lot of chewing gum in their mouths. That could be the biggest thing in the cafe business since neon, but I guess it wouldn't be the same.

Nothing ever is.

A Busy Place
(February 28, 1990)

One time the local newspaper got him to advertise.

"Daddy said he'd never do it again," recalls Sue Meyer, the former Suzanne Whiteside of Gonzales. "There were just too many people."

Not that her father, Boothe Whiteside, didn't have enough customers as it was at his little cafe on St. Francis Street in Gonzales, where it's said as late as the 60s that he would do 1,000 hamburgers and 70 pounds of chili on a Saturday.

Maybe that was during cotton picking but, nevertheless, it was a busy place just as it had been during her grandfather's time before him, and she says her grandfather, James Edward Whiteside, would let the cafe fill up and then close the doors. When it got empty, he'd let it fill up again.

He had paid $600 for the cafe in 1926.

Mrs. Meyer, who was at the chili cook-off at the Land of Leather Days in Yoakum with husband, Jim, says her granddad came to Gonzales from Temple and originally had a fruit stand where he did a good business selling bananas in an alley beside the cafe building.

"He did so well he bought the building," she says, "and started making hamburgers and chili."

The Whiteside chili was so popular they had people asking to buy the recipe, but she says her dad has kept it a secret to this day.

The Meyers stopped in Gonzales on their way back to

Austin and called in some prices from the menu as it was when Whiteside closed the cafe in 1979. Hamburgers were 90 cents, chili buns .85, a bowl of chili $2.35, ham sandwich $1.30, two eggs and sausage $1.85, and coffee .21. That compares to a 1943 menu that they have that shows hamburgers at 10 cents, hotdogs a nickel, Irish stew .25, small chili .15, large chili .25, two eggs .15, small T-bone .50, hamburger steak .25 and five cents for coffee or a soft drink.

Mrs. Meyer says when her father closed the cafe in 1979 that he left everything the way it was in the building and it's the same today.

"The calendar is pulled off to May 5, 1979," she says.

Her father will be 85 years old next month.

"He had the cafe for about 20 years from 1959 until he closed it in 1979," she says, "but he always said he would open it again someday."

She helped in the cafe from the time she was in the third grade until she was graduated from high school, and then again some in 1976.

"We pressed all our own hamburger patties," she recalls. "Dad would fry them just a few seconds and then flip them. He would take them off for awhile, and then he'd put them back on. I don't know what purpose he had in doing it that way. Every morning at 4:30, I got to chop the onion."

She said the whole family would get up and go to the cafe where they opened at 5 a.m.

"Me and my brother, Ed, who still lives in Gonzales, my dad and my mother, Lucille. Mother had worked in the cafe for my granddad and that's where she met my dad."

Mrs. Meyer says her parents lived in Cuero for some time after they married and worked at the cottonseed oil mill, until her grandfather died and they returned to Gonzales to run the cafe.

"When daddy got older he still opened at 5 a.m. for the morning business," Mrs. Meyer recalls, "but due to his health he would close from 11 a.m. to 1 p.m. since he could no longer handle the crowd."

He never sold beer, she says, nor French fries which he considered too much trouble.

There was business enough anyway, without adding fries to the menu.

During the Depression, she says her grandfather was known for doing a bit of advertising.

"He'd fry onions, and open the windows."

Would remind everyone in town the Whiteside Cafe was open for business.

Palace Cafe
(April 2, 1987)

Order a high ball at the Palace Cafe in Shiner and that's what you get.

Chili and stew, mixed.

Hugo Schwabe says lots of folks around there like it that way, and he recalls old Doc Williams used to come in regularly from his office upstairs over the adjoining corner drugstore to have his high ball.

Schwabe was behind the bar last Friday when his wife, Kamela, was away from the cafe for awhile, and was recalling that he met her there in the cafe something like 43 years ago when he was working on the road between Shiner and Moulton, or was it Hallettsville? He's been in the road building business for years, and had someone coming by that afternoon to look at some equipment he'd put up for sale.

Dennis Caka and I stopped in to see the place, and thought maybe we might have a hamburger, but we were too late for dinner. Outside of stew, chili, hamburgers and the like, Schwabe says they also serve one kind of dinner each day, and from what I've heard it's worth being there on time.

The Palace Cafe has a huge, fancy back bar that was worthy of the finest saloons during the days when it was shipped by train to the young town of Shiner, now celebrating its 100th birthday. The bar was brought in about 1906, after Bill Zappe had rented the place from the developer, William Green. The bar came from Chicago, but was originally from Germany. After Zappe, Hugo Pohler had the place for 20 years, and Weldon Schultz had it when he was drafted in 1942. He wrote his mother to sell it, and that's when Mrs. Schwabe bought it.

We stopped back in later when she was there and talked to her about how long she'd been in the cafe, said 44 years all total. She's seen lots of customers come and go during all those years, and says she's seen them put sugar in their beer, chase it with raw eggs, mix it with red soda pop, and eat raw potatoes so they'd stay sober. Said there was a fellow who rented an upstairs room for a time who would come down in his housecoat and pajamas, eat about three dozen raw oysters before retiring for the night.

Mrs. Schwabe says she has never had any real trouble at the cafe, and never had to call the law in 44 years.

She's the former Kamela Mikes.

Schwabe says he can remember as a young boy standing in the door watching five men standing on the counter selling beer and booze as fast as they could move it. That was the day before prohibition, and folks were stocking up for a long dry spell.

Then there was the cotton picking seasons, when the cafe would be so crowded one could hardly get in the door, and he says hands waiting for work or in town for the weekend would be sleeping on the streets like dogs at night.

There was also a funeral home two doors down for a long time, and it brought in some good business. It was customary to hold wakes, and some would come in to brace themselves for the long nights with the body, others would need a lot of coffee to stay awake.

Been a lot of changes over the years, but the Palace

Cafe is still pretty much the way it used to be, with the big fancy highback bar and walls decorated with horns various members of the family have contributed over the years, including a huge tusk from an elephant that Schwabe says his brother, Willie, brought home after it took him three days before the other elephants would let him have it.

The Palace Cafe is a good place just to stop in and look around, have a cold beer or soda pop, a one of a kind dinner, or a high ball.

Mixed with a Shiner twist.

Frills Wanted
(February 9, 1983)

I'm the kind of person who will drive out of my way to get a good hamburger, that's one with real meat in it, kind of greasy on the outside, with lots of goodies on the inside.

I'm talking about the kind we used to get at practically any truck stop or good eats cafe along the highway, at the little eating places around the schoolhouses, and at the street corner diners in the larger cities.

They were real hamburgers, with mustard on them, plenty of tomato, lettuce and pickles, and big round slices of Bermuda onion. There are still places that make them like that, but they are becoming few and far between, and now I hear there is something coming on the market that is called a no-frills hamburger, just meat or something that passes for it placed between two halves of a bun without any goodies at all on it.

I can't see how anyone would want to go out and eat something like that, but from what I hear they are going over big with the young folks of the microwave generation, the connoisseurs of junk and fad foods seem to have an appetite for anything cheap and quick. My parents kind of thought the same of me when I was eating those greasy burgers at the little stand near the high school in my hometown. They couldn't understand how I would prefer something like that to the balanced meals in the cafeteria.

Now we're told the hamburger comes close to being a balanced meal and they are even serving them at school, although I'm sure they are nothing like the ones we were accustomed to. If they were cooking anything like that in the cafeteria we'd be able to see the smoke, smell the hamburgers cooking as we drive by.

About half the young people I know won't even get close to an onion, and you'd think a little mustard was going to kill them, and real grease is something they don't even know about.

I guess it's all in what you develop a taste for.

When I get a hamburger that doesn't come up to my expectations, I always think of something that a former *Advocate* reporter, Jim O'Brien, once did. He went into one of the fast food places that make all their burgers just alike, got his order and lifted up the bun to see what was in it. After deciding there wasn't enough onion to suit his taste, he asked if they would give him another slice, offering to pay extra for it. He was politely told that was against the rules, that they couldn't deviate from their formula.

He paid the bill, politely took the hamburger to the nearest garbage pail and dumped it.

Walked out a satisfied customer.

II

MORE EATS

Turtle Soup
(February 10, 1985)

First things come first if you're making turtle soup. You start with a turtle, for one thing.

"A soft-shell turtle," says Edna Brandt of Yorktown, who's known for good turtle soup.

First heard of turtle soup about five years ago when Carolyn Stauss told me about it, said I ought to look up Mrs. Brandt sometimes when I'm out that way and I've been intending to ever since. I even had her on my New Year's list of people to see for a couple of years, then kind of forgot about her and her turtle soup.

Then last Sunday during the trail ride at Meyersville, while I was trying to warm up by the fire at Joe Migura's store after watching the riders arrive, I overheard two women talking about me, introduced myself and one of them said she was the lady who makes the turtle soup. She told me a little about how she goes about it.

Mrs. Brandt says she originally got the recipe from the late Edward Schulze, who lived out in the Dobskyville area where she grew up. He was a big fisherman and knew all about such things as making turtle soup.

"The hardest part is killing the turtle," she said.

I can understand that, a turtle isn't one to stick his

neck out for something like that, and that's understandable. Once the neck is out, it's not all that hard to figure out the rest, she says.

Mrs. Brandt says you can skin the legs like a frog, take the rest of the meat out, and keep the top shell.

"You throw away the bottom shell," she says. "Some people make the mistake and try to use that."

There is something like seven different kinds of meat in a turtle, and she suggests frying the bulk of it and eating it that way.

"Fry the heck out of it," she says. "It's better than any kind of meat you can eat."

She says it tastes a little like fish.

The soft shell and the bones with meat left on them then goes to make the soup, but first the shell must be properly cleaned.

"It'll have slime on it like catfish," she says. "Boil it in real hot water and peel that off. I use my hands."

Then, she says, put the shell and the bones in water and boil until the meat is done. You won't need a lot of water to start with, and she says it doesn't take long.

"Not unless you get one of those real old babies."

When that's done take the bones out, along with the shell. Cut the soft gristle from around the shell into squares and return that to the pot with the meat that's left in it, along with any meat that's cut from the bones. Throw the rest of the shell out.

"Then you throw in everything except the kitchen sink," she says.

In other words, whatever you might normally put in soup, and then some.

"The more the better," she adds.

Last, and most important, she says to add some sweet cream right before it's ready to serve. The more you add the richer it gets, might give it a taste test when you think you've added enough.

I never attempt to give recipes as such, being an eater and not a cooker myself, but this should give some idea of how she goes about it, and from what I've heard about her turtle soup it's worth a try.

"A lot of people don't like it," she says, "because it does have a flavor all its own, kind of like fish soup. If you like fish you'd probably like it, if you don't you probably won't."

Her husband Pete says he likes it, but Mrs. Brandt says their kids never cared much for it.

Wouldn't mind trying it myself sometime, if I happen to catch a turtle that will cooperate.

One willing to stick its neck out.

More on Turtles
(March 26, 1985)

Thought about Edna Brandt's turtle soup again last week when talking to V.T. Kallus.

Kallus mentioned having turtle during World War II with the islanders on New Caledonia, and I gathered from the way he described it that they bake the turtles something like the Hawaiians do their luau pigs. Course they've got big turtles over there, big green sea turtles which the islanders catch napping and flip over on their backs. That pretty well takes away from a turtle any place it could go.

"They're pretty good eating," according to Kallus.

Then I got to talking Saturday with Liebert Schulze of Yorktown, who mentioned Mrs. Brandt's turtle soup. Mrs. Brandt got the recipe from the late Edward Schulze, who lived out in the Dobskyville area where she grew up. Edward was one of Liebert's brothers, and they and Mrs. Brandt are cousins if I got it right, their mothers having been sisters.

Schulze said it was originally his mother's recipe, and he says his wife, Elenora, still makes it sometimes when he finds the right kind of turtle. He said finding a turtle can be a lot like floundering, that they will bury themselves in the sand with only their head and sometimes not even that sticking out. He said it's best to wade in behind one in a creek or river and then reach down and grab it from the rear and stand on its head being careful not to let it scratch you with its hind legs. Turtles are pretty good scratchers.

Soft-shell turtles are used in making soup, and he says it's true there are different colors and textures in the meat. It has different tastes like chicken, beef, pork and whatever else you might want to make of it.

He said the recipe goes back to at least the earliest years of the century, when his mother was still single and cooking for Gus Lenz of Cuero, who he recalls was sheriff of DeWitt County later on. At the time, however, he said Lenz had a cafe or something like a boarding house in a big old two-story home that stands on Highway 87 between Cuero and the bridge over the Guadalupe River. At the time, Schulze said the road west still went to old Clinton across the river and passed right by the house.

Must remember, that was in the very early 1900s, at the latest, since his mother was born in 1879 and he figures she was in her early 20s when she was the chief cook there. There was a lot of traffic in those days along the road, Cuero having been established only about 30 years before as the western terminus of the Gulf, Western Texas and Pacific Railroad. As a railroad terminus, Cuero had quickly eclipsed nearby Yorktown, which had been an important stage and wagon train stop on the road from Indianola to San Antonio.

Yorktown got a railroad in 1886, but by then Cuero was already an established shipping center and a lot of produce continued to be moved across the Guadalupe by wagon, along with herds of cattle from west of the river. It was a good spot for an eating place there on the road where the old house still stands along with the oak tree in the yard.

Schulze said when they passed that way his mother would always point it out, because on that tree was where she said they'd hang the turtle shell on the days when they were having soup, when they were lucky enough to have a big turtle from the nearby Guadalupe River. That way those on the road would know they were having something special.

Couldn't find turtle soup just anywheres.

Poke Salad
(March 24, 1982)

Bill Allen of Crescent Valley called Friday morning to let me know he had some poke spotted.

Had promised that he would, once the weed began to poke through this spring, said he had a pretty good bunch of it located. He had read where I mentioned nobody had ever pointed it out to me, that I'd never tasted the stuff even though I'd heard a lot about it.

Do believe I received more response from the columns on poke salad than on anything I've ever written, both from those who can remember when it was the only greens on the table and those like myself who are mostly curious about it.

Shortly after mentioning it, I noticed an article in some gardening magazine about poke salad, written by Carroll Abbott of Kerrville. It was Abbott who persuaded the Legislature to set aside the fourth Saturday of each April as Texas Wildflower Day.

What he had to say about poke is pretty much what I'd heard before, that it's delicious when prepared right, if you like greens.

Allen took me out behind the Victoria DuPont plant where we found some of it growing in a ditch beside the road, beneath a tree.

He said to be sure and parboil it, preferably twice. That simply means to boil it good for several minutes and pour off the water, then do it again.

A person should gather only the young plants, or new growth at the top of a plant. The plants we gathered were about 10 inches tall. Both the leaves and the tender stems are good to eat.

The old plants, and the root of the plant, contain phytolaccin, a slightly narcotic, cathartic substance that works as a slow acting emetic in large enough doses, from the way Euell Gibbons describes it in his book, "Stalking the Wild Asparagus."

The substance is actually poisonous and the seeds of the plant are highly poisonous. Gibbons wrote that his mother made a medicine out of them that she gave the kids to purify their blood when they had boils or pimples, also used the root in chicken water, supposedly would keep the chickens from getting a disease.

Walked in with the paper bag full of greens and the wife got curious, asked me what I had in it, told her I finally got me some pokeweed.

"You don't expect me to cook that stuff, do you?" she asked.

Told her I did and she said she would, although she didn't seem real happy about it. When she got to cutting it up, she recognized the smell, said it was called inkberry where she grew up. It's also known as garget and pigeonberry.

Birds evidently carry the seeds because it's often found growing in yards where it never grew before. Once you know what a plant looks like it's easy to recognize, the stems have a purple hue, the leaves are shaped like a lance and are about the color of spinach and looks much the same.

After parboiling it twice, the wife fixed it pretty much like spinach. It's good to use bacon drippings, but we didn't have any, so she used margarine instead.

Found the taste very much to my liking, the greens a little like spinach, the stems more like asparagus. Both being among my favorites, I would have to say poke salad tastes ever bit as good as I'd been told, and especially with brown beans and cornbread.

Could live through a Depression on something like that.

Scratching Around
(May 31, 1984)

A lady on Main Street was telling me about her mama's chicken feet.

I was scratching around for something to write, but she's the one who won't ever let me use her name, got something against seeing it in print. Don't suppose she will mind me talking about her mama.

She said her mama would cook the chicken feet and it would give them something to chew on while the rest of the meal was cooking, which reminded me that my mama used to do something like that when we still butchered chickens. I don't have a real clear vision of just what she did with them, but I do remember seeing chicken feet in the pot and her gnawing on them. Mama always cleaned off her chicken down to the bare bone anyway, but she seemed to think there was something special about the feet. The lady on Main Street tells me they're about the best part of the chicken.

I never have liked chicken all that much anyway, except in soup with lots of rice. Come to think of it, I believe that's where mama used to put the feet, along with the neck and maybe a backbone or something like that, enough to flavor it good. A person could get two meals out of a chicken that way, fry or bake the good parts and put the odd ones like that in a soup, and mama never did believe in throwing anything away that she could use. She also liked to gnaw on the neck a lot which was always her favorite part of the chicken.

Maybe women just develop a different taste for chicken, being in the kitchen with them so much. Spent most of my time with chickens out in the barnyard, and I've seen what all they eat. Made me wonder at times how we can eat them at all, but must admit there are times when I do go for a good mess of chicken livers or that piece with the pulley bone. That's always been my favorite piece.

After I got home from talking to the lady on Main Street about her mama's chicken feet, I turned on the television to watch the evening news and they announced Russia had developed an amphibious chicken. Wonder why they'd go and do a thing like that, right off I can't think of a single reason why anyone would want an amphibious chicken, it's difficult enough to find eggs as it is the way they are now. I suppose it would make for a cleaner chicken, unless they're like a mudhen.

Would think they'd been better off developing a chicken without feathers, know some of our scientists worked on that once, but don't recall ever hearing how far they got with it. It would be an ugly chicken, but it sure would be practical and wouldn't take so long to get one dressed if company should drop in unexpectedly for Sunday dinner.

I might suggest a lot of things that would be more practical than that Russian water chicken, like a double-breasted one, for instance. That way there would be enough white meat to go around. They might also consider developing one with four legs instead of two, would sure save a lot of fussing at the table for families with more than two children. I must have been an odd child, never cared that much for the drumstick myself.

Sure could have used an extra pully bone at times.

Sourdough Bread
(March 6, 1986)

Rudy and Alice Laitkep looked as fresh as if they had just gotten up to milk the cow.

"We got in at four o'clock this morning and were here at seven," he was telling me, at the Settlers' Day where they had an exhibit on cream separating and butter churning, along with kraut making, homemade soap, and even sourdough.

Sourdough is something I want to learn more about.

Laitkep and his El Campo Melody Boys had played the night before at Rogers, close to Temple, at Seaton Star Hall. That's out around my papa's old stomping grounds, and anyone who has ever spent any time at all around Bell County has heard of Star Hall. The Melody Boys play that old-fashioned polka and waltz music that folks out around there like so much.

In their own life-style, the Laitkeps have managed to retain a lot of the old ways in modern times, and I mentioned once before that they're among the few people around who still milk a cow regularly. Laitkep has a Guernsey that gives two gallons a day.

We didn't get to talk a lot, because there was so much activity around their booth, with folks asking all kinds of questions about some of the things they do. It's amazing how much attention you can attract with a little butter, and there was also a steady stream of folks across the way at the Community Center watching the Victoria Extension Homemakers, who were churning butter in several different ways. They were also handing out samples of buttered bread. It's hard for me to believe now, but what we called "butter bread" didn't impress me a whole lot when I was a kid. I preferred sweet cream, with sugar on it — what we called "sugar bread," now that was a real treat.

Laitkep was showing me a big crock that he uses to make his sauerkraut, and said when he was a kid his mama used to put him in the crock to stomp the kraut. While she poured off the juice each time she would hold him under one of her arms, tip the crock with the other hand, then put him back in and let him stomp some more. He said she'd always wash his feet real clean first, and afterwards they'd really be clean.

"I had the cleanest feet in town," he says.

Their sourdough starter was something of particular interest to me, since that's really something you don't see too often any more. It's not something you can buy in the store or just make up on a spur of the moment, since you have to start with some starter to begin with. Sourdough is a mixture of flour and water which has been allowed to ferment in order to trap natural yeast, and as the mixture is used it is constantly replenished with the addition of more flour and water. I've read that J.C. Hunter at Abilene has some sourdough starter that's been kept going for more than 100 years and is supposed to be the oldest in the state.

Mrs. Laitkep says their sourdough originated in the family with her grandmother, Mary Rebecek, who came over from Czechoslovakia in 1883, but when and where she got it isn't known. It was passed on to Mrs. Laitkep's mother, Millie Wagner of Shiner, and then on to her. It's definitely been around for awhile, but sourdough is that way when it's taken care of.

Put some freshly churned butter on a piece of sourdough bread and you've really got something substantial, a little sauerkraut on the side and maybe a thick piece of home cured ham, now we're talking real food.

Have an idea the Laitkeps know how to eat.

Nose Knows Cheese
(March 11, 1980)

Stink cheese is something that lives up to its name. Not that it's not good.

It is like some other cheeses that smell up a storm but have an appealing taste, each in its own way. What was probably more appealing about this one at one time was that it could be made quite easily at home, and a lot of it was.

Don't find many people making it any more, but that's not because they don't like it. When people gave up the milk cow, they gave up a lot of things.

I really don't know much about stink cheese, but Frances Hartmann of Yorktown, told me a little something about it.

Now it seems different people call it different names, like rotten cheese, for instance. She says a more polite term for it is hand cheese, having something to do with being able to roll it up in a ball by hand after its ready.

The reason there are a number of names for the cheese is that it was popular among several of the nationalities that first settled this area, and each had a particular way of describing it.

Mrs. Hartmann, who is the librarian at Yorktown, says it takes about three days in warm weather to make the cheese and really get the full flavor.

The cheese is made from clabber, something I always found kind of tasty but haven't seen a crock full since I was a kid. The clabber is hung up in flour sacks so the whey will drip off.

Then the curds are pressed real good to get all the whey out, otherwise she says the cheese will turn out bitter.

This gives a general idea of how it is made, but not the whole story of course. There are matters of timing, seasoning and things like that. The cheese can even be cooked to make sort of a spread.

Not long after we talked about the cheese, I was having a cup of coffee with a friend when the waitress brought over one of those little containers of cream. I never had paid much attention to them, not using the stuff myself, but for some reason I happened to notice this one. Maybe it was because I still had the cheese on my mind.

I couldn't help but notice that it was labeled as a nondairy product and a coffee whitener, whatever that means. The stuff I took to be cream wasn't cream at all. I tasted it. It didn't taste like cream either.

Seems like it is getting harder and harder to find anything that's real anymore, or even to tell the difference.

That's one thing about stink cheese.

There was never any doubt about it.

Snouts for the Snooty
(June 27, 1984)

If you've got dinner guests coming who are a little on the snooty side, and you don't know what to fix, let me make a suggestion.

How about snouts?

That should impress them, probably talk about it for a month of Sundays afterwards, because it's sure not something they could get every day, not even in the finest of restaurants. I'm told that a good meal of snouts is all it takes to get rid of the worst case of falutins, will even bring down a nose that's stuck on the ceiling. Know a couple of people I'd like to have over, if I can find the snouts.

Now some folks are going to think I'm just joshin, as they say where snouts are on the level, but I'm not. I look at it as a public service to spread the word about things like that, and I'm grateful that Leon Raaz and I got to talking on the farm tour about some of the things folks used to eat that you don't see much anymore, like pig snouts. Most of the snouts are hidden away today in weiners and stuff like that. Even before folks mostly hid them in headcheese or souse, but there were some who fixed them a la carte, so to speak.

Raaz says he's had boiled pig's snoot before and it's pretty good eating, lot of meat to it and not so greasy like hog hocks and some parts like that, and goes good with cornbread. I've also heard snouts are good roasted.

It's just another one of those things like chicken feet, which people were more inclined to eat before we got so stuffy about our food. Raaz says his mama used to make a stew out of chicken feet, which are easy to prepare for cooking, just cut the toenails off, wash the feet good and throw them in the pot. We're talking about feet from a young fryer of course, wouldn't want them off an old rooster or a hen.

Raaz, who farms at Wood Hi southeast of Victoria, was telling me that his mother, Ida, also used to make her own hominy, would cook the corn for a day or so with a little bag of wood ashes in the water to get the kernels to puff and peel. He said that was better than using lye, that the potash will seep out of the bag and do the job just as well. He says it should be cooked in a porcelain enamel or a cast iron pot, or perhaps stainless steel.

Raaz said they'd pick ears of corn with the biggest kernels to make their hominy, and the old yellow dent variety was ideal for it. He was telling me about another old variety farmers used to plant that had the ears way up the stalk, that was especially good in the river bottoms.

Kind of got off the subject, but had pretty well said all we know about pig snouts.

If you do have some company coming for dinner like we mentioned, would imagine you can still find a butcher who'd put some back for you, if you tell him what you need them for.

That you've got some snooties coming to dinner.

III

SAUERKRAUT

Kraut Stompers
(April 12, 1983)

Came back from the Wharton County Fair and told the wife that I found out how to stomp sauerkraut.

"You don't stomp sauerkraut," she said.

"Some do," I replied. "Folks used to do it all the time, in the old days."

"You don't stomp sauerkraut," she said. "You use a stick."

"I'm telling you," I said. "I met some people who still put up their sauerkraut by stomping it."

"You don't stomp sauerkraut," she said.

Must be the Indian blood in her, can't always get her to accept the ways of the white man, can only imagine what some of her ancestors on that side of her family must have thought about the strange habits of the German and Czech settlers when they first came over. Stomping sauerkraut probably looked to them like some sort of dance.

What we are talking about here is putting sauerkraut up in a crock, not canning it in jars like most people do now, folks didn't have a lot of jars back there when most of the stomping was going on. Now some did mash the cabbage down with a stick, that's true.

I suppose the advantage of using one's feet is that you get a good even distribution of weight, without beating up the kraut so bad. Like Japanese massages, let one of those girls walk around barefoot on your back and it can feel pretty good, but it would be a whole different story if she took a stick to you. Think the same principle is involved in stomping sauerkraut, in some way. Do know you don't want someone too heavy to do the job.

Mary Jane Balcar of El Campo says their children have all stomped sauerkraut, the younger ones taking over from the older ones when they became too heavy. She says her husband Victor has been putting up sauerkraut like that for years, with the help of their children, Sandra, now 17; Linda, 16; Clarissa, 15; Brenda, 13; and Jeffrey, 10. Can guess who's doing the stomping now.

They also sometimes put pickles at the bottom of the sauerkraut, says by the time they eat down to them that they are really delicious. The old-timers probably did it that way because they didn't have but one crock.

We got to talking about sauerkraut during the barbecue judging at the fair. Wayne Popp had brought along a jar of kraut for the judges to use in between bites, clears the tastebuds. It wasn't stomped kraut, but he and his wife, Shirley, did put some up that way awhile back, mostly to show their daughter, Kendra, 9, how it used to be done. She got to do the stomping, and from what I could gather in talking to her it wasn't all as much fun as it might seem to be. Stomp around in a crock for a couple of hours and it can get to be drudgery, be enough to make you want to pick up a stick and get after it.

Did pick up a little advice on sauerkraut stomping that I'll pass on, should anyone decide to try it. It's advisable to wash your feet before doing it. Toenails should also be cleaned.

At least once a year.

Clean Feet
(June 12, 1984)

Joe B. Liska of Runge comes from a long line of sauerkraut stompers.

"I won't make sauerkraut if I can't stomp it," he says. "Using a post to pack it down is too darn much work."

Met Liska over at the school reunion at Runge last Saturday, had about 900 gathered there at the new VFW Hall, and as far as I know he was the only one in the bunch who still stomps sauerkraut, thinks he may be the only one in Karnes County who still does it that way.

I know some folks who used to do it, and Wayne Popp over in Wharton County was showing a picture around the fair there earlier this year of his daughter stomping some, but they just took it mostly to show how it used to be done. Wayne's way too big to stomp kraut anyway, unless it was cut real thick and put in a hot tub or something like that.

Liska says he's been stomping kraut since he was a little kid, about 10 years old, or thereabouts. He learned it from his dad, Joe Sr., a Czech immigrant who evidently had learned how to do it in the old country from his dad, and Liska says he still uses a homemade cabbage slicer that was handed down from his father's grandfather.

"I can take a hundred pounds of cabbage and slice it in 20 minutes," he says. "I put a No. 3 tub under it."

Liska says it takes about 110 pounds of cabbage to make 10 gallons of kraut, or about 40 quarts. Said he made 10 gallons not long ago, and that he'll see to it that I get a quart.

"I washed my feet good," he assured me.

He does make some for other folks on occasion, but says he has been asked before and when the person found out how he does it that was all there was to it. Wouldn't matter to me, unless he'd been out in the chicken house gathering eggs right before, think all the salt would about take care of anything else.

"As I throw in the cabbage I put some salt in," he says. "The way I check the taste is by the water."

The water comes from the stomping, and Liska says he starts out by filling the crock with cabbage and stomps that down, repeats the process until he gets the crock full, then lets it ferment until it's ready to put in jars.

"In warm weather it takes about two weeks," he says, "but the best time to eat it is when it's about half fermented, right out of the crock."

He seasons it with caraway and dill, and the only water he ever adds is that which he puts in the top of the jar to neutralize fermentation.

Someday I'd like to go out and watch him do it, Liska says he's not hard to find, lives on the same farm where he was born and raised about 3 ½ miles north of Runge off the Helena Highway.

"Ask anybody in Runge," he says. They will give you good directions to my house, and most times I'm in town anyway."

He's a retired farmer, but still has a little moonlighting job as veterans service officer for Karnes County, but other than that he mostly specializes now in making kraut, jerky and mustang grape wine, which sounds like a pretty good combination to me.

Had planned to ask him if it takes any certain rhythm to stomp kraut good, to get it even all through the crock, but we got to talking about something else and I forgot.

I'd think a little polka beat perhaps.

Dishing It Out
(April 6, 1993)

A lady walked up and said she never tasted sauerkraut.

Told her she hadn't lived.

I had stopped at the sauerkraut booth at the Matagorda County Heritage Day in Bay City, which was being operated by Eldrid Schilhab, Virginia Carr and her cousin by marriage, Lilly Carr, and Albert Zalman, who was busy working the kraut cutter.

Zalman is an old sauerkraut stomper, having had that job when he was a kid.

"Mama would wash my feet good with homemade soap," he says. "We'd put up two half-barrels of sauerkraut a year."

Kids were often called upon to stomp kraut when families put up a lot of it, as they often did in those days, sometimes with sliced cucumbers or potatoes in it, or pickles at the bottom.

They were serving it fresh from the crock Saturday, dishing it out like ice cream, and I settled there for a spell to munch and talk kraut.

I like good sauerkraut, especially just out of the crock that way when it's good an' crisp, not like the stuff you buy in a store that's stringy and overly sour.

It's supposed to be sour, but not like that, and anybody who has ever tasted the real stuff will never again be satisfied with anything less, and it kinda grows on a person after awhile like Spanish moss.

I pretty much grew up on it myself, like many German and Czech kids, and I can't remember when I didn't like sauerkraut although I have an idea there was a time when I didn't, since like most kids I didn't always like my vegetables.

Sauerkraut was about the only vegetable that farm families had at times, except maybe for beets and canned carrots, and at that age I sure didn't care for red beets and thought carrots were something rabbits ought to be eating.

Zalman was saying they made 50 pounds of kraut for the Heritage Day.

"I was afraid we wouldn't have enough Germans and Bohemians to eat it," he said.

They were dishing it out pretty good, however, and not too many turned it down, but then I suppose everybody can't have a taste for sauerkraut.

Zalman and Mrs. Schilhab were telling how simple it is to make, using a recipe from "the old Ball canning book" which calls for four tablespoons of salt to five pounds of finely shredded cabbage, with a little fresh dill mixed in.

"Pack it in a crock, cover it and forget about it for two weeks," Zalman says, "except for skimming off the top about every three days."

It can then be eaten from the crock or canned.

"Just bring it to a heat and put it in the jars," he says.

Sounds simple enough, and the only really hard part is shredding the kraut and that didn't look too hard the way he was doing it with a 100-year-old kraut cutter that belonged to Mrs. Schilhab's grandmother, Mrs. Joseph "Clara" Besetsny of Schulenburg.

Mrs. Schilhab was born in the old Besetsny home on Highway 77 North, the daughter of Beno and Agnes Besetsny.

Zalman got his sauerkraut expertise at El Campo, where his parents Anton and Albina Zalman lived and where he later operated a Gulf station at Church and Mechanic street for some 33 years.

While we talked, he had worked a head of cabbage down to the core, which he calls, "the Bohemian apple."

Some people take the core out, but he likes to leave it in for a little more crunch. That's what makes sauerkraut good, when it has a nice crunch to it.

More the better for munching.

The Easy Way
(June 16, 1993)

Asked Johnny Zavesky if he stomps his kraut.

"No, I sure don't," he said.

Zavesky then explained how he does it the easy way.

"You just pack it in a good jar and put a tablespoon of salt to a quart, and fill it full of tap water. Just hold it under the faucet."

Sounds like something I could even do.

Zavesky and another notable sauerkraut maker, Joe

Liska, had both donated some of their best for the auction at the St. Anthony's Catholic Church Feast in Runge.

Liska still stomps his kraut by foot and recently told the "Country Boy" columnist W.C. Reader in Karnes County just how he does it, in a big "old-timey crock" that has been filled with sliced cabbage.

He said the next step is to take off your shoes and wash your feet good, but watch what you use as a disinfectant or it can destroy the flavor of the finished product.

One has to stomp it thoroughly for about 15 minutes to separate the water from the cabbage.

Add salt as needed, and put a clean rag on top and let it ferment for about 14 days before putting the kraut into jars, leaving about an inch of space at the top to be filled with boiling water to stop the fermentation.

There's a bit more to it, but that is basically the way foot-stomped kraut is prepared, but Zavesky says that's just too much work.

"I take the work out of it."

Zavesky just retired as a longtime barber in Karnes City, having been there since he got out of the service in 1946, but started barbering way before that in 1937 in Hallettsville and is a member of the barbering Zavesky family that included six brothers who became barbers and four nephews.

He was the last of the ten to retire.

I had heard that he had left the farm to become a barber because he got tired of working behind the exhaust of the mules on the farm, but he says the oldest boys had left home to be barbers and the youngest were still too young to do much in the field so his dad, Joe, just quit farming.

Zavesky had also barbered at Moulton, Westhoff and in San Antonio in his earlier years.

As for making kraut, he learned that from his mother, Rosie, and says after running tap water over the sliced and salted cabbage all you need do is "heat your lids and seal it."

If a person is going to make kraut either way, I would suggest they talk it over first with someone like Zavesky or Liska, who has the experience to know just how long it should take before it is ready and that sort of thing, which can even depend on the weather from what I understand.

I do know, according to what Liska had told Reader, that if any of the lids are bulging in about three days that you might as well throw those jars out.

Sure can't eat soured sauerkraut.

IV

BARBERS

▽▽▽

Shoveling Bull
(August 31, 1993)

Story around Hallettsville is that it took a couple of extra days to bulldoze all the bull out from under the building.

There at the old Zavesky Barbershop where the Peoples State Bank was tearing down the building as part of an expansion project on the south side of the courthouse square.

It's not only hair that stacks up at a barbershop, and Charlie Zavesky always kept that shoveled up pretty good in the 52 years that he was a barber, something like 27 years in that particular building. His dad had it for 15 years before, which adds up to a lot of hair and bull, both being by-products of barbering.

Zavesky hung up his clippers on May 1 and was one of the last of the barbering Zavesky family to do so, another being an uncle, Johnny, over at Karnes City, who quit barbering in June.

There had been six barbering brothers, including Charlie Zavesky's father, Charles, plus four in the second generation of Zavesky brothers.

The old-style barbershops are getting fewer and farther between every year, but were once popular gathering places not only for haircuts, but for a shave, shine and local news as well.

Notice I didn't say gossip — that was reserved for the beauty parlors where no self-respecting man would have been caught getting a haircut as so many do now in the unisex barber and beauty shops that have become so common.

But, then, neither did the women deal in bull.

Bull was reserved for the men, and I suppose over the years a whole lot of what was left behind did collect under Zavesky's barbershop where he tells me they also discovered an old well that he had never known was there.

"Right in front of my chair," he says. "I could have thrown someone right into the hole."

It was a shallow well, or possibly an old-time cistern, the way he describes it, only about eight feet in depth at the most, and seven or eight feet across at the bottom, and maybe four feet at the opening in a shape something like a jug.

"I heard it belonged at one time to the East Hotel," he says, "and was like a wishing well."

The north window gave a good view of the courthouse square and all the goings on around it, and the barbershop even became a gathering place several years ago for the movie stars who were in town for the filming of "The Best Little Whorehouse in Texas."

Zavesky had autographed pictures of Burt Reynolds and some of the other stars hanging on the walls.

But it wasn't movie stars for which the Zavesky Barbershop will best be remembered, but simply as a barbershop of the old style, not all that different from the one where his father first started cutting hair in Hallettsville back in the 1920s.

His dad was barbering on the west side of the square when Zavesky first started as a shine boy.

He would later attend the same barber school in San Antonio that his father had attended, Lewis Barber College, and received his license on Jan. 7, 1941.

Within a couple of years he was cutting hair with the U.S. Navy.

He was also among the reserves called up for Korea.

During his 52 years in barbering, Zavesky saw haircuts go from 40 cents to $5, and when he first started a man could get a shave for a quarter, or a haircut and a shave for 60 cents.

In talking to him about his retirement, on Friday

evening at Gibbe Gerdes and Kenneth Henneke's annual birthday stew and turtle soup supper, I got to thinking how much hair Zavesky must have swept up over the years.

Can't quite shovel bull the same way.

Bowl Haircuts
(February 1, 1980)

There was a time when I was a little tyke that I recall some discussion in my family as to whether my hair should be cut at home or not.

Haircuts didn't cost much, but the family was looking for every way it could to save a few cents. I didn't like the idea because I had visions of dad putting a bowl over my head and trimming around it. Somewhere I'd heard that was the way it was done.

As it turned out, I got to go to a real barber, and it wasn't long after that the GI haircut came in style. Didn't need a bowl for that, a good pair of sheep shears would do. Guess dad didn't think of that.

The only part I didn't like about the barbershop was having to sit on that board across the arms of the barber chair. It was a sure sign you were growing up when they didn't have to use the board anymore, and when they started using some lather on you. Those were days when a razor cut meant the barber had made a mistake.

It was only recently that I found out dad had aspired at one time to be a barber, and there's a man over in Cuero who he practiced on.

Rueben Birkelbach was only four years old then, and dad was a farmhand working for Rueben's father in Littlefield where the Birkelbach family had moved from Central Texas.

It was around 1928 and dad wanted to go to barber college. He was from around Rosebud himself, and when he wrote home about it the family talked him out of it.

Barbering jobs were hard to get, and if you got one you didn't get much. Haircuts were two bits at the time, and not everyone got one when they needed it.

Birkelbach was in Rosebud recently to see an uncle and ran into an uncle of mine who told him dad now lives in Cuero, so he looked him up when he got home. It was the first time they had seen each other since those days in Littlefield, and they did a lot of reminiscing.

One of dad's jobs with Birkelbach's father was riding one of the horses that pulled the reaper. That's the only way there was to guide the thing, which was pulled by two mules and three horses. He also recalls threshing maize in a big sandstorm without ever stopping.

"We'd come home and you couldn't tell what color we were," he says.

I have run into a number of people who think he was with the newspaper here before me. That could have something to do with haircuts. There were many years that I wore a flat top, back before I got a razor cut on top and quit shaving below. Guess there are those who think that was my father.

That would make me my own son.

The one who never did like to shave.

The one who usually needs a haircut.

Board a Tradition
(July 2, 1981)

Lois Reeves says I wasn't the only kid who didn't like the board.

"Kids still resent it, promote them as soon as I can," he says. "Sometimes sooner than I should, makes it difficult to cut their hair."

Know I never liked to sit on the thing, made me feel like a kid.

After getting off the board, the next step toward manhood was the day the barber lathered you up good and shaved around the edges, when that happened a boy knew he wasn't always going to be a boy. Barbers do that with fine clippers now, must take some of the joy out of growing up.

The board is still there, however, fits right across the arms of the chair like it always did, noticed some of them are padded now and look a lot more comfortable than the one I had to sit on.

Reeves has a little barbershop in Bloomington, has been there since the 50s, but has been cutting hair since 1926, says when he got started the electric clippers were nothing more than a hand clipper with an electric motor attached. It got the job done, which was all that mattered. Got clippers now that even suck up the hair as they go along.

A lot of kids have sat on Reeves' board.

"When a kid first came in whose daddy had sat on that board, I began to feel old," he remarks. "Now I'm cutting the hair of grandkids."

I have found memories of the barbershop in my hometown where a kid could learn a lot if he kept his ears open and his mouth shut while the grown-ups were talking. There isn't much that ever happens in a community that doesn't get aired thoroughly in the barbershop.

Never have noticed much difference in barbershops anywhere, they all seem pretty much the same, all remind me of the one in my hometown of Ballinger where I was graduated from the board.

Had a barber pole out front, kind of like the one at Reeves' shop — red, white and blue, going round and round. There is a lot of history behind those things, like they weren't always red, white and blue, that's the American version.

The barber pole came about in olden times when barbers were permitted to do minor surgery, mainly blood letting and tooth pulling, and would sometimes hang their bloody bandages out front. The barber pole was devised as a way to let people know that surgical services were available on the inside.

Red and white stripes originally represented the

bandage with which the barber wrapped his patient after letting blood. There was a symbolic basin beneath the early barber pole, representing the bowl in which the blood was caught.

Glad barbers weren't doing anything like that when I was a kid.

Couldn't have got me near that board.

Cackling Sounds
(September 6, 1987)

Said he first thought it was a frog or something.

"I don't have any chickens," explained James C. McCormick, as we talked about something a little out of the ordinary that happened awhile back at his little barbershop on Raab Road near Nursery.

McCormick has been barbering since 1933.

"Except for four years I put in the Marines," he says, "and I barbered in there, too."

Barbered in New Zealand and other places in the Pacific, while serving in the Marine infantry on Guadalcanal, Guam, and other hot spots during World War II, got to talking about how they'd catch water in their canteens with banana leaves when it was raining, and it rained a lot.

He was also recalling a dairyman in New Zealand who turned his cows out and made his barn into a laundry, said the man also had a Ford truck that burned wood, which sure goes to show that's not a new idea. He said the fellow would give the soldiers rides into town, and pass a can around so he wouldn't have to account for it.

Warren Tomasich, who lives on King Drive, was doing a bit of resting at the barbershop, and J.R. Smith, who lives on McCormick Drive, came in for a haircut. He's originally from Speaks and was recalling a big thunderstorm there one time when two men riding by the school got struck by lightning. He said a bolt ran down a tree and hit one of them in the head, killing both the man and his horse.

McCormick grew up near Nursery and went to school there and at Patti Welder High School in Victoria, said back when he was a kid you could still see rows of stumps where the old Onderdonk Nursery used to be, which is how the community of Nursery got its name. He said a couple of big hailstorms back there did the nursery in, and except for a few of the trees and the stumps there wasn't much left of it even then.

He did most of his barbering in San Antonio over the years on Blanco Road, having his own shop there for 27 years, but about three years ago decided to move back to his old home country and opened a little shop on Raab Road.

"I just felt too good to quit," he says.

McCormick said he was cutting Wilbur Cummings' hair the day they heard the noise. Cummings also lives out that way, off the Levi-Sloan Road, and he'd come over in his pickup truck. When they got to looking to see what was making the cackling sounds, they found one of Cummings' chicken hens outside the barbershop. They got to looking and found she had a nest with several eggs under the tool box in his pickup truck.

"I have a throw net, but the chicken was too fast," McCormick says, "and it flew into the garden."

They finally gave up on catching her, until that evening when Cummings returned and parked his pickup near the hen.

"Late that evening, him and her both came over, and they sat on the steps here for awhile, until the hen jumped into the pickup, then they got in and took off for home."

Chicken was ready to go by then.

A Cut Above
(August 8, 1993)

Carlos Delgado wanted his children to have an equal education.

Around 1916, prior to the time his first and second oldest sons were to start school, the Victoria barber and boot maker began efforts to have the Mexican-American children integrated into the local school system.

Prior to that, Victoria had separate schools for Mexican children, dating back to the beginning of the state's public school system, and this separation continued in many communities well into the middle of this century.

In a paper done while he was a student at Southwest Texas State, Steven Davis, son-in-law of Abel and Cecilia Delgado of Victoria, described how Carlos Delgado's efforts ended school segregation for students from the Mexican-American community.

Abel Delgado is one of the younger sons of Carlos and Hersilia Delgado and a third generation barber in Victoria.

His two oldest brothers, Daniel and Charles, were among the first to attend the integrated class of 1917.

In general, the segregated Mexican schools were inferior to the Anglo schools, often with teachers who themselves were barely educated, as Davis points out in his paper. When Delgado learned of these conditions, he decided that he wanted his children to have an equal education.

A respected businessman from a family in which education was an important concern, he enlisted the pastor of the Mexican Presbyterian Church, a Rev. Acevedo, to assist him in changing the system so the Mexican children could attend the better Anglo schools.

"Unlike the segregation of the blacks," Davis notes, "the segregation of Mexican-American children was not based on constitutional or statutory grounds. Instead, it came about as the result of school board or administrative policies."

Delgado and the Rev. Acevedo then approached an influential Anglo businessman and community leader who was sympathetic to the plight of the Mexican-American children, and while he elected to remain anonymous, he assisted in drawing up a petition to be presented to the Mexican-American community.

No one would sign it, however, fearing retribution and the possible loss of their jobs, but Abel Delgado says the Anglo benefactor then suggested they present it "in the name of all Mexican-Americans in Victoria."

The board accepted the petition, which reads as follows:

"To deny integration for the Mexican American's child imposes a lifetime hardship on a discrete class of children not held accountable for their disabling status. The stigma of illiteracy, through the lack of proper teachers, will mark them for the rest of their lives.

"By denying these children a basic education, we deny them the ability to live within the structure of our civic institutions, and foreclose any realistic possibility that they will contribute in even the smallest way to the program of our nation. And, whenever our nation calls upon them to serve this country, they will not be able to give full service capabilities."

With World War I heating up, it was a plea with added substance.

Davis was unable to find evidence of the petition in the school records, or even any mention of the decision to integrate, nor could he find any newspaper account of the action — but he was also unable to find any references after 1916 to any "Mexican School."

There was, however, an effort mentioned in 1920 to again segregate the schools. The measure failed.

The man responsible for ending segregation for the Mexican-American students came to Victoria from Mexico in 1902 as a young man with his family. His father, Agustin Delgado, set up a barbershop at 206 S. Bridge.

The family later built a house and barbershop at 208 W. Constitution, where the Victoria County jail is today.

Carlos Delgado married Hersilia Garcia of Inez in 1909, and there are nine of 14 children living, all of whom attended integrated schools in Victoria, thanks to their father's concerns in 1916.

While during his younger years he was both a barber

and a boot maker, Carlos Delgado continued to barber until the age of 92 in 1972, and died in 1987 at the age of 102.

Abel Delgado has continued to operate his father's barbershop, known now as the Six Flags Barbershop at 1206 E. Juan Linn, and believes it could be the oldest continuously operated family barbering business in Texas.

It was there, one recent afternoon, that we talked of his father's accomplishments as he was busy barbering.

How Carlos Delgado helped all Mexican-American children in Victoria to get a better education.

Barber Boss
(May 5, 1981)

Boss Mills was busy sweeping rain off the sidewalk.

He's swept that sidewalk a few times since moving to Karnes City in 1920, fresh out of barber school. Been in the same barbershop ever since where he has seen a lot of changes take place. The rain brought back memories of days when wagons sometimes got stuck out front.

"Them days there were three gins, three stores, three doctors, and on Saturdays several fist fights," he recalled. "Stopped a good many fights myself, didn't want to see friends get messed up."

When Boss arrived, there were three barbers in the shop, but he had the first clippers. They hung on a wire and were passed from one to the other, would sometimes get so hot they'd have to let them rest awhile.

Each morning a group of regulars, about a half-dozen usually, gather on the old wood bench, then head down to the drug store for coffee and to catch up on what's happened since the morning before.

Historian and author Bob Thonhoff of nearby Fashing has dedicated his latest book, *The Texas Connection With The American Revolution*, to Boss Mills and his barbershop gang, past and present.

"Got some of my best information out of that barbershop," Thonhoff says. "Some of it I couldn't have gotten anywhere else."

Recalls he was once trying to locate the site of a lake that existed in the Karnes City area during the Spanish period. He heard a duck hunting story in the barbershop about a lake somewhere around Panna Maria that some farmer had drained and found it was the one he was looking for.

He asked Boss once if he knew of two small peaks the Spanish had aptly named, somewhere around Smiley. Boss knew of them by other names, but they turned out to be the ones Thonhoff was trying to locate. Boss grew up in Gonzales County, knows that area well.

Thonhoff, a native of Colorado, says he acquired his first love of Texas in the form of a wife from Coy City, the former Vicie Balser, but his second love of Texas and its history was initially acquired in Boss Mills' barbershop.

"It was people like Boss Mills and that grand group of guys that sold me on this part of the country," he says.

Thonhoff is completing his 25th year in the school system at Fashing, where he's the elementary principal. Among his other historic writings was a book co-authored several years ago with Robert S. Weddle entitled *Drama and Conflict: The Texas Saga of 1776*. It was then that he became interested in the way Texas contributed to the winning of the American Revolution.

He presented the first copy of his new book to Boss Mills.

Noticed an old cardboard sign up on the wall with prices of the barbershop services listed — haircuts $1.50, flattops a quarter more. Found out the sign might be old, but the prices are current, although Boss says he doesn't cut many flattops these days.

Boss doesn't particularly like to get his name in the paper, but guess it can't always be avoided, not when a man has cut hair in one spot for more than 60 years, gets a book dedicated to him, passes his 90th birthday, and keeps right on working. Man like that is bound to attract some attention.

Looked like he has a pretty good handle on using that broom, but guess he's had practice over the years, both out there on the sidewalk and in the barbershop.

Can't imagine how much hair he's swept out from under the chair.

Thick and Thin
(April 19, 1987)

Frank Polasek walked out of the cotton patch and became a barber.

Sixty years ago and he's been barbering ever since, although he says now he only does it when he feels like it.

"If I feel pretty good, I stay there pretty regular," he says. "If I get tired, I go home."

He barbers in Hallettsville, just off the courthouse square a bit, across the street from the old Cole's Theater where he barbered before building his own shop about 1966.

Polasek celebrated his 80th birthday and 60 years of barbering last Sunday during a barbecue at Wied Hall, which was almost like an old barbers convention with his Uncle Louis Matula there, who he first got started with, and Ben Appelt, who he barbered with back in the 30s.

"When I started," he recalls, "most shops had one clipper on a stand that was rolled from one barber to the next, the old Racine clippers that worked something like a sheep shear, but about the time I got started we started using the little vibrating clippers."

That's the old clippers that used to get so hot, that a lot of us can remember, especially when they'd touch the back of the neck.

Polasek was born April 11, 1907, at Salem, near

Ezzell, where his parents, John and Mary Polasek, had bought a place in 1898, and he recalls there was only a cow pen and a calf pasture between their house and the school. It was in 1927 that he went to Lewis Barber College in San Antonio for four weeks, after he convinced his dad that was what he really wanted to do. Boys in those days stayed at home longer than they generally do now, and Polasek says he was a little reluctant to ask if he could go, until one day he and his dad were out picking cotton and the right opportunity presented itself.

"I never was much of a cotton picker," he recalls. "I could pick maybe 200 pounds a day, and dad might pick four or five hundred, and that day we were picking three rows together, and I was picking one and he was picking two."

Polasek said his dad had about 40 pounds picked to his 20 when they were down the row pretty good, and stopped to rest awhile.

"I said, 'Daddy, what bout me going to that barber school,'" he recalls, and his daddy pulled up his picksack and sat on it and spit. "You can't pull no damn cotton no how, you might as well go do something else," he said, and that was the end of his cotton picking days.

After he finished barber school, Polasek said his dad loaned him some money and he bought into a barbershop at Shiner with an uncle, Louis Matula, so he could have a job, and stayed there about four years, after that barbered for a few months in Dallas and then about four years at Kerens in Navarro County. Polasek said he came back to Lavaca County and raised tomatoes for a year on the home place, but froze out twice and then had to sell what he made for a cent and a half a pound, so he had enough of tomatoes and went back to barbering for Ben Appelt at the Theater Barbershop in Hallettsville. Appelt sold out and went into the real estate business, and he continued on there with Frank Zavesky until about 1966 when he built his own shop across the street.

Polasek lives 11 blocks up the Schulenburg Highway

and says he walks to town every morning and has been doing that for 15 to 20 years now. At noon and in the evening, he says his wife, the former Mary Bell Jalufka, comes after him, except sometimes he'll walk home if she's busy, but says he doesn't like to do that because by then he's tired and doesn't like to crowd himself.

"It's wonderful when you can be there and work when you feel like it," he says.

Another barber, Joe Raska, pinch hits for him some when he doesn't feel like it, and Polasek says he may get him to do that more often now if he will.

The Polaseks were married in 1935, and they still live in the same home he built before they got married. They have two children, a daughter, Mrs. Garland "Carolyn" Kolle of Victoria, and a son, Pat Polasek of Houston.

Polasek said times were hard back in the 20s when he first got started barbering, when haircuts were 30 cents and shaves 20 cents, and that he started several times to pick up his tools and throw them in the street, but stuck it out anyway.

He recalls there were some busy times back there when the women started getting their hair cut short, during the Flapper days of the 20s, and he said there would be hair nearly a foot deep on the floor. He said once he was being so careful cutting a pretty little girl's hair he clipped her ear and the blood started shooting out, but he got it stopped and told her how sorry he was about it, and she kept coming back after that to get her hair cut.

"I never lost a customer," he says, "but that was about the most embarrassing thing that ever happened."

In 60 years of barbering, Frank Polasek has cut many a head of hair, long and short, and in between.

Through thick and thin.

V

HOME REMEDIES

Sweating Out Colds
(January 22, 1982)

Feel like I've got a watermelon between my shoulders.

A cold can sure get the head stuffed up like one, rest of me feels even worse, throat scratchy as a chicken yard at feeding time, chest feels like it's been kicked by a mule wearing new shoes.

My feet even ache, probably in sympathy for the rest of me.

It is absolutely amazing to me how a little old germ about .000002 inches in diameter can cause one to feel so bad, got that measurement out of the *Old Farmer's Almanac* should anyone wonder how I know such things.

Since I haven't been able to get out much the last couple of days — kinda hard to interview someone when you're coughing in their face — I've been catching up on my reading, found an article in the *Almanac* that seemed most appropriate to the occasion, on cures for the common cold.

Someone asked me what I'm doing for mine, actually I haven't done much of anything, cold seems to be getting along pretty well on its own. Not much a person can do for one except try to give oneself a little relief, did take a couple of cold tablets that the wife gave me, but they didn't seem to do all that much good and I'm just not much for taking pills of any kind.

Did get me some chicken soup, always seems to help me more than anything, even heard something on television the other night that research indicates there is some merit in the old belief that chicken soup will give some relief from a cold, think perhaps a lot of the old treatments, remedies and so-called cures might have some merit.

Some of them I do have a hard time swallowing like one I read about in the book *Texas Folk and Folklore* suggesting that red chili peppers swallowed whole like pills will cure a cold, have an idea that would only make a person forget he had one.

Might go along with the goat tallow, horehound, or even the tea made from broomweeds.

When I was growing up mama had her own way of dealing with colds, the chicken soup was part of it, but when it came time for me to go to bed when I was down with one, she would rub my chest good with Vicks, rub under the arms, on the back, on the bridge of the nose, under the nose, across the forehead, then she'd make me stick some up my nose, and finally she'd put a big wad on her finger and stick it in my mouth, put me in a flannel shirt and stick me under enough covers to thaw out an Eskimo village.

If I was lucky and there was some whiskey in the house — mama never believed in it for any other purpose, so there seldom was — she might make me a hot toddy with sugar water and a touch of cinnamon, give that to me before the Vicks treatment.

The whole process is known as sweating out a cold, and although I've heard some doctors say that it's a good way to get pneumonia, it always seemed to work pretty good in my case. It's funny that so many things seemed to work back then that are now looked on with suspicion, although I'm sure some of it is justified.

Folk medicine was an important part of our culture

when I was growing up, and I'd like to hear more about it since I don't remember all the things we used to do. Used kerosene a lot, I know that, and bacon fat.

Onions were big when it came to colds, my wife says her mother used to make a very effective cough syrup by heating honey water over sliced onions, adding a little vanilla or lemon extract to the mixture for flavor, something like that can make a kid get over a cough pretty fast.

Her grandfather had a simpler remedy, put a drop or two of kerosene in a teaspoon of sugar, made the kids swallow that. The boys had to be real careful if they were just beginning to smoke.

I'd always heard of kids having to wear a bag of onions or garlic around their neck to ward off colds, but never saw that practiced myself, would think that would certainly keep people with colds away from a person.

I see mention of one cure in the *Old Farmer's Almanac* that I'm not about to try.

No way am I going to stand on my head in a bucket of water.

Take This
(February 5, 1982)

Our comments about home cures reminds Mary Filley of some her daddy used to mix up to give the kids.

One she particularly remembers, with an ugh.

That was a concoction of molasses mixed with powdered sugar. She says her dad would make them each eat a plate of it, that she always hated to see him start to mix it.

"Every bite he'd have to whip me," she recalls. "It had an awful taste."

She's not exactly sure what it was supposed to do for them, but he seemed to think it would keep them healthy and always gave it to them in the spring.

She said her daddy also mixed a hot toddy, which wasn't so bad. It was made with lemonade — "with enough ginger in it to burn the devil out of us." He'd give that to them when they caught cold, then put them under heavy covers to sweat it out.

Mrs. Filley was telling me that her daddy once had a horse that got bit by a rattlesnake, said the Mexican cowboys told him to cut Spanish dagger and place the spikes around the bite. The horse got well.

I've read of that cure before, the wound should be made to bleed freely with a sharp knife, then tops from a half-dozen blades of Spanish dagger should be stuck under the skin around it, left there until the next day.

The rattlesnake story reminded me of something Henry Novak told me when I was at his place near LaSalle, mentioned that his favorite dog had been bitten by a rattlesnake not so long ago, got over it. Reason a dog can survive getting bit on the head, he says, is because they can't get to the wound to lick the poison.

Mrs. Filley also mentioned how they used kerosene to wash out wounds, especially nail wounds in the foot. It's amazing more people didn't die of lockjaw. We lived on a sheep ranch for awhile before I started school. The place was covered with mesquite trees and I was constantly stepping on thorns, had many a wound washed out with kerosene myself.

I remember hearing a story once, might have been out around the Cowboy Reunion at Stamford, about an old-timer who'd been coming across the country in a covered wagon and somehow a rattlesnake got him on his back side. He kept right on going, poured some kerosene in a dishpan and put it on the wagon seat, then sat in it. By the time he got where he was going he was well, suppose it could have happened.

Mrs. Filley told me a story that did happen, about 1940, when she was working at De Tar Hospital as a nurse. A man from Shiner was brought in who'd been working on a construction project at one of the local banks and developed an allergy to cement that caused him to break out in a rash. It wasn't anything real serious, not so serious at least that some of his buddies didn't slip in a case of Shiner beer for him. Might add that he was Czech, had the accent.

There was another young nurse there from Louisiana, who worked the shift before Mrs. Filley. The next morning when Mrs. Filley relieved her, the girl was bubbling over with excitement, couldn't wait to tell her all about the new patient.

The man from China.

Some Friends
(February 11, 1982)

A lady at Retama North nursing home tells me she has five boyfriends out there.

She says there is Will Power, who is always around in the morning to help her get up, then she walks around with Charlie Horse, eats with Arthur Ritis, has a drink afterward with Al Kaselzer, then watches television with Ben Gay, an old friend who sometimes has to take care of Arthur Ritis when he gets a little rambunctious.

Not going to tell you who the lady might be, wouldn't want to make the others jealous, but will say she was among a group we met with to talk about home remedies after our recent column on the subject.

Just happened to appear the same morning they had a discussion group going on the same subject, part of the National Council on Aging Humanities Program. The group got together again later for our benefit with Mary Stegman, discussion leader, and Beverly Broderick, extension assistant at the public library.

Those who met with us included Delia Mueller, Ella Grasse, Mildred Bridewell, Bessie Ivins, Lee Christian, Justa Torres, June Sutherland, Clara Floyd, Lucille Galloway, Josephine Hollub and Hattie Hanshaw.

Could be Delia who has all those boyfriends, but we're not telling.

The ladies got to reminiscing about some of the old home cures, like asafetida bags that mothers used to hang around the necks of their children to keep the colic away. Lucille, Clara, Bessie and Hattie all said they could remember wearing the foul smelling substance made from the roots of several plants.

Josephine said she could remember some neighbor children and cousins having to wear the stuff, around the waist instead of the neck, said her family lived so far out in the country that she wasn't likely to catch anything herself.

Bessie, Clara and Josephine all recalled cough remedies made from rock candy, whiskey, lemon juice and such, including camphor gum. A mixture with camphor gum was also heated and placed on the chest with a flannel cloth, Hattie recalls.

Another chest remedy, according to Clara and Josephine, was turpentine, hog lard and coal oil, heated and rubbed on, covered with a cotton cloth or flannel rag, believe it was Clara who said the mixture was made with a half-cup of lard, a half-teaspoon of coal oil and six or seven drops of turpentine.

Clara said mustard plasters were used for pneumonia, when the doctor gave up on saving her youngest, she kept up the treatment with success.

Bessie, who raised five children, recalled that when a baby had a cold she'd hold it up to the fire and warm the feet, also that some relief for earache can be achieved by holding the stem of a pipe up to the baby's ear, letting the warm smoke go in. Hattie said camphor in a warm pancake was another good remedy for earache.

When a heating pad was needed, Delia said she wrapped hot bricks, Clara said a stove eye is also good, or a fruit jar filled with hot water, seem to recall that one myself.

They all said some of the old remedies worked surprisingly well.

There was one, in the book they were using, that none of them seemed to recall, supposedly for chest congestion. The fat of a polecat can be rendered and eaten, just two or three spoonfuls is supposed to bring the phlegm up, but then just thinking about it might do it.

Their discussion leader didn't know what a polecat was until they got to that part of the book, said she never heard them called that where she's from, believe she said Illinois. Hadn't heard about a lot of the old remedies either.

Some I don't remember myself and others I'd just as soon forget, like anything involving castor oil.

Somewhere during the discussion, Ella said what she needed was something for her rheumatism.

Might find herself a boyfriend.

Someone like Ben Gay.

Cure Milked
(February 16, 1982)

Thought I'd milked home cures for all they're worth, then met up with Monroe Kovar out on the trailride and he told me one that about tops them all.

He says Grandmother Kovar would make a tea out of sheep droppings, that and some kind of plant, for the croup. Said she wouldn't use droppings out of the barnyard but would get clean ones from the pasture. She'd boil the stuff together, then strain off the tea.

Kovar says he doesn't know if he was ever treated with it, but presumes he probably was at some time since she talked about how she did it.

Think that one has to rank along with the polecat fat for chest congestion.

I also found out some more about that molasses and sulphur mixture, what Mary Filley had told me about, but didn't know what exactly it was supposed to do, just that it tastes awful. Bessie Ivins tells me it was given to ward off the malaria, or whatever caused chills and fever.

Mrs. Ivins was one of the ladies participating in the discussion group on old ways at Retama North nursing home. Recall the first time I ever met her, she was 80 years old at the time and had entered a rocking chair marathon during the Victoria Sesquicentennial Celebration in the fall of 1974. Understand she has entered walkathons, other things like that, since then.

Wish I had a little of her energy right now, maybe something for this sore back I got tilling up the garden. Wonder if that polecat fat would work for that, some of it might be congestion from all the fog we've been having. Sure hope I don't get the croup.

One lady called me and gave me a remedy for whooping cough, said it cured her son after three doctors had given him up when he was six weeks old, in 1933. She said on old lady told her to get some mare's milk and give it to him.

She said a fellow who ran the golf course in the town where they lived just happened to have a mare with a foal. They managed to get enough milk to feed the baby with a medicine dropper, and it wasn't long before he began to show some improvement.

She doesn't know just how much the mare's milk had to do with it, since there were a lot of people praying, too. Talked to her son about it, he didn't seem to particularly want the story spread around.

Can understand that.

Still had to milk it for what it's worth.

Time Tested
(September 10, 1993)

Some of the things we did in the way of home remedies would make a doctor turn white as a hospital sheet today, but most of those old remedies were time tested and folks just didn't run to the doctor with every little thing that happened.

I was out at Our House, a local residence care facility, one day last week and was talking with the residents about some of the old remedies they remember, and Florinda Sierra, the youngest member of the group who just happened to be celebrating her birthday, was telling how her mother uses spider webs to stop bleeding, especially for bad cuts on the head.

While I've heard of that before, I've never seen it done, and she says it works pretty good.

The youngest resident of Our House, having been born in the early 1950s, she says that when she was growing up on a ranch near Meyersville that her family mostly took care of its own medical problems.

"Everything ever happened to us, we would take care of it," she recalls.

The other residents grew up before mid-century when home cures were the rule rather than the exception, like Mina Rau Moehrig recalls how a copperhead snake once bit one of her sisters while she was feeding cattle.

"She got as far as the gate and passed out," Mrs. Moehrig says.

"Papa cut the bite open with a razor and sucked the blood out, and then soaked the wound in a gallon of coal oil."

She says it took a couple of weeks for her sister to get over it, but Lillie Rau Spreen is 92 now and living in San Antonio. They grew up around Brenham.

Minnie Munselle Holly, originally from Brownwood, said her mother never had a doctor in the house except for once "when one of the boys broke his arm."

"He fell off a horse, or a horse fell on him," she says.

That was one of the more common accidents back in what we think of now as the old times, and the only time my father was ever in the hospital as a youngster was when he'd been kicked by a mule.

Opal Caraway Weisse recalls how she used to hide the asafetida bag from around her neck in a prickly pear patch on the way to school, so she wouldn't have to wear the smelly thing all day, then she would retrieve it on the way home.

Asafetida bags were supposed to keep germs away and were commonly worn by children.

She was born at Leesville in Gonzales County, but

grew up at Cuero.

Raymond Schultz, born and raised about a half-mile from Little Chicago near Yorktown, was recalling an old German tonic that was popular when he was young, and while children would only get a dose of it, the old folks would drink it with their meals.

It was called Oppenkrater, or something like that, and was sold by individual dealers.

Tonics and other such patent medicines were popular up until the 1950s. I particularly remember Hadacol, which some said was called that because they had to call it something.

One resident of Our House, Armanda Cavazos Gonzales, says her dad came from Spain and didn't believe in the old remedies, but they had a doctor friend in Brownsville who would come by to check on them.

She became a nurse, studying at the TB sanatorium near San Angelo, and worked in her profession for close to 50 years.

Thinking back to the time when Hadacol was so popular, I remember how many jokes were being told about it, like one Mrs. Weisse remembers about "an ol' girl who couldn't read or write."

"They gave her a bottle of Hadacol," she says, "and now she's teaching school."

Sometimes humor is the best tonic of all.

Ant Liniment
(March 6, 1996)

Alice Laitkep was explaining how she makes her ant liniment.

She and her husband, Rudy, were participating at the Settler's Day, something they enjoy doing each year for the Victoria County Senior Citizens Association, and the ant liniment was just one of the things they had with them.

Of El Campo, the Laitkeps like to do things the old way, including milking their two Dexter cows, making butter and cottage cheese, butchering their own hogs, making lye soap, plucking goose down, and baking sourdough bread — to name just some of the things they do.

The ant liniment was something that I hadn't heard about before, and Mrs. Laitkep explains it is an old home remedy for charley horses, bruises, insect bites, sprains — just about anything external requiring an anodyne.

She says it will soothe an irritant and is especially good for insect bites and stings.

Eight yellow jackets once stung her on the middle finger of her right hand and, having an allergic reaction, she says the finger swelled up something terrible and a doctor told her that it would never go down.

"He said that I would just have to live with it," she recalls. "It was so painful, I couldn't explain it to anyone."

So, she doctored it up with her ant juice.

After about a week, she says the swelling went down and she couldn't even tell that she had been stung.

She learned the remedy when she was growing up at Moulton, the former Alice Wagner.

"We had an old neighbor who treated himself," she recalls, "and I just happen to remember how he did it."

The liniment is rather simple to make, she says, since all it takes is a bunch of ants and some regular rubbing alcohol.

First, of course, one has to catch the ants and it does take quite a number to have enough.

"I use my fingers," she says. "Real fast, and so far I haven't gotten stung."

She learned it is best to stop up the ant hole first, otherwise the ones being caught send out some sort of signal and all the others scurry back into the hole.

Her husband says one can put honey in a jar with a stick leading up to it and let the ants get stuck there, but Mrs. Laitkep says that's just too sticky for her.

"And, you catch a lot of other things," she notes. "I just want red ants."

She only uses the big harvester ants that are more commonly known as red ants.

When she gets enough, she covers them with alcohol and lets them soak undisturbed for two weeks.

She then strains about a half-inch of the concentrated ant juice into a small half-pint jar and fills it with alcohol.

It is then ready to apply as needed.

Feeling Fine
(June 14, 1983)

Joe Tymrak doesn't look like a man who once thought he was on his way out.

After playing an hour or more of lively music on his key accordion at a reunion at Hallettsville for descendants of Frank and Rosalie Janak, he told us what he did to cure himself of a bad ulcer back in the early 50s.

"I went to the doctor," he recalls. "He told me there wasn't anything he could do for me and sent me home to die."

Tymrak said on the way home from the doctor's office he asked his wife to stop at a liquor store, so he could get himself a bottle of muscatel, figured he might as well die happy. He said the man that sold him the wine had tears in his eyes when he heard the news.

Tymrak said he drank some of the wine, and on the way home gave his wife his billfold, told her how he'd like to see the kids raised, wanted to be ready when the time came. But he wasn't quite ready to give up either, when he got home he ate a bar of yeast and drank a little more wine, slept awhile and repeated the process.

The next morning he went to work in the store, operates Joe's Place in Jourdanton, on Highway 97, where he started the combination cafe, store and beer joint in 1938, same year he joined the volunteer fire department. He's still with both, in fact he's the oldest active member of the fire department and has been dispatcher for over 30 years, blows the siren right from his house.

After finding out he was going to die, Tymrak said he didn't eat much for about three days, but stuck with his yeast and wine treatment. After he got to eating better he kept up the treatment in varying degrees until his system seemed to be in working order again. He returned to the doctor three months later for an X-ray, found that his ulcer was gone, and says by then he could eat sauerkraut, or anything.

Tymrak asked the doctor why he couldn't prescribe the treatment. The doctor told him that he couldn't do that, had to stick with what he was trained to do, dispense prescription medicines, and that he couldn't give out homemade prescriptions even if they did appear to work.

Didn't matter to Tymrak, he was feeling fine, said he made up his mind that he was going to live or die and was glad to be living. Got that twinkle in his eye to this day of a man who enjoys life, and he can really spice it up a bit with the accordion, had a whole crowd gathered around him singing at the reunion. His wife, Jourdine — believe he said she was named after the town — is a descendant of Frank and Rosalie Janak. Her mother was Theresa Janak Dornak, one of their children.

Tymrak said a Mexican fellow who trades with him came down with ulcers once, used to come in and order toast when his wife had chili and the kids were eating hamburgers. He asked Tymrak for the cure, said he wrote it out for him, but put down that he was no doctor, just in case. The man went out and got himself a gallon of muscatel since he lived pretty far out of town and couldn't get back in as often as would be required to complete the treatment.

"He was down to 139 pounds," Tymrak recalls. "Now he weighs 220, and he's healthier than I am. After he got well, he cured his father-in-law.

Sometimes when he comes in looking for Tymrak, he asks where his doctor's at, both get a laugh out of that.

Got something to laugh about.

Colic Cured
(August 29, 1984)

Pappy Thompson telling about the time he ate the apple peels got me to thinking about some of the old remedies for colic.

That's a tummy ache, for you youngsters who might not have heard of it. We still had the word when I was little, but by then we had some medicines for it and the home remedies weren't being used as much as before, which I'm not complaining about after reading up on some of them. Some of the treatments for colic seem to me to have been worse than the pain, certainly were enough to make a kid think twice before coming down with the same thing again.

One old cure was a tea made from the white lime of chicken droppings, also I understand some old-timers used sheep droppings, just take two at bedtime and call me in the morning if it hasn't gone away. Believe I could get to feeling better real quick. Course colic was a baby problem mostly, and I guess they could only squall about it.

Some used asafetida bags tied around a baby's neck to keep the colic away, and asafetida and whiskey in milk or water was often used if that didn't work, also a drop of kerosene at times. Soot, ginseng and baking soda were other ingredients in old-time colic mixtures. No wonder some of the old folks are so tough.

Pappy Thompson's not all that old, whatever 1917 from now equals, and he looked pretty fit to me when I was talking to him on Indianola Beach awhile back, although he tells me he's always had a small stomach and a little heart and thinks the apple peels might have had something to do with that. He is old enough to have gotten in on some of the treatments that were pretty well gone by the time my generation came along, and I'd sure never before heard anything like the one about the apple peels.

"I was still in diapers when it happened," he recalls. "We were at Grandmother John Raska's house at Hope."

Thompson said his mama, Mary, and his Grandmother Raska were peeling the apples to make pie, had a porcelain enamel dishpan under the table in which they were dropping the peels, and he snuck under there and filled himself up. Now that's a sure way to get a good stomach ache, know when I was little my mother would always peel the apples for me to make sure I didn't get one, and after Thompson told me what happened to him I'm kind of glad she didn't let me have the peels.

"I was turning blue," he recalls. "Grandpa Raska warmed up some water in a foot tub and put me in it. Then he got some water boiling in a big wash tub, and he floated the little tub in the big tub, turning it so that the water would get hot gradually. He had me covered up with a pillow slip or something, so I'd inhale the steam."

Thompson said he might have been little, but he can remember how hot that water got, but it cured him. Evidently the old man cooked those apple peels right in him, or at least got them hot enough so they wouldn't ferment or do whatever it is they do to give a kid the tummy ache.

Understand Thompson was one steamed kid before it was all over.

VI

SCHOOL DAYS

Clearing the Air
(April 30, 1995)

Miss Willis was telling about hygiene.

She asked why people took baths, and one little student, Velcie Fitzgerald, spoke up.

"If we didn't," she said. "We'd stink."

It was just one of the memories of the country school at Midfield that several former students were recalling during a recent reunion with one of the teachers, Eunice Willis, who taught there from 1926 to 1928, when she was just a young teacher beginning a career that spanned 46 years in the classroom.

A resident of DaCosta, she joined several former Midfield students, including Nellie Nygard Cornelius of Edna, Bill Richardson of Midfield, Margaret Anderson Bunge of Garwood, and Lucille Melbourne Bolling of La Ward, for dinner at The Dock restaurant in Bloomington one recent evening.

At the time that Willis taught third and fourth grades there, Midfield had a four-teacher, nine-grade school. The farming and ranching community is located 25 miles southeast of Edna in Matagorda County.

Richardson showed up for the reunion by bringing his former teacher an apple.

"I never had the money when I was in her class," he commented.

As a young teacher, after graduating from Patti Welder High School in Victoria and attending summer school for teachers in San Marcos, Willis started teaching in the fall of 1922 at the Leona School on the Kolle Ranch. After a year there, she taught at Placedo for three years before going to Midfield.

She taught at a number of other country schools later, including Casa Blanca between Wood Hi and Telferner, also at Lake Placedo, and retired from teaching in 1969 after 23 years at Flour Bluff.

"I enjoyed teaching at Midfield a lot," she recalls. "The kids were good kids."

Her former students remember that she always told them that one of the most important things to do was read.

While she was one who believed in maintaining discipline in the classroom, none could recall her ever giving anyone a spanking, although there was once when Richardson thought he had come close to getting one.

"Lucille and I were acting up," he recalls, "and she (Miss Willis) sent me to get a switch."

When he came back with it, she told him to roll up the legs of his britches.

"Then, she told me to go sit down," he says. "I sure thought we were going to get one."

Some of Nellie Nygard Cornelius' memories of her school days at Midfield have to do with riding horseback three miles to school and back home each day.

"In the afternoon, during the winter, I would have to face the north wind," she recalls, "so I would turn around in the saddle."

She had a good horse that didn't mind her riding backwards and knew the way home.

It wasn't as far as Lucille Melbourne had to ride, however. She and her four sisters rode double some five miles both ways.

Margaret Anderson Bunge was a couple of grades below Nellie, Bill and Lucille, and therefore didn't have

Miss Willis for a teacher. Her father, Halley Anderson, had the grocery store at Midfield at the time, and an uncle, Ernest Anderson, ran the post office.

In 1929, the school burned down, and Richardson says the fire was thought to have been started by the heater, a heater for which he remembers having to carry coal. That was a chore the boys enjoyed, because it got them out of class for awhile.

For a time, school was held in some old store buildings, until a new one, which even included stalls out back for the horses, was completed the following year.

During the afternoon following the previously mentioned discussion on hygiene, and odors, Richardson and Raymond Hale were dragging off a dead cat when the boys got in an argument after Hale said the cat stunk.

"Don't say it stinks," Richardson admonished him, thinking back to what they had learned that day. "It has a bad odor."

Seems that's not the way Hale had heard it, thinking Miss Willis had said order instead of odor. First thing the next morning, Richardson says he asked her, "If she hadn't told us to say odor."

Just wanted to clear the air.

Real Stinker
(March 10, 1995)

Bill Hajek stunk up the school.

Back when he was a student at Industrial Junior High School in Lolita, where he now teaches science and computer literacy, Hajek had a close encounter with a dead skunk while marching with the school band.

"Clinton Schutt stepped on it," he recalls, "and it spurted all over me."

The band was practicing marching along a road near the school for one of its many appearances.

"We were always going to festivals and other events," Hajek says, "and wore laced leggings and army helmets painted yellow."

Fortunately, that day they were in their school clothes.

He says the band director was a Mr. McGuffee, who wore thick glasses and held the music close to his face, and naturally he wasn't overjoyed with what had happened, nor was the school principal, Buford E. Carnes, who just happens to be Hajek's neighbor now.

Hajek says after he and his wife, Maggie, a teacher's aide at Lolita, moved next door to Carnes, he asked the retired principal if he remembered the skunk incident.

"He did," Hajek says.

He was telling about the incident last week during a free period at the Industrial Junior High Author's Fair, where writers, artists and others in various fields are brought in to discuss their work with the students.

I just happened to end up in Hajek's room, which I thought smelled pretty good for a science room.

It was my second time to participate in the Author's Fair, and like last year, I left with good feelings about the younger generation. I couldn't have asked for a more attentive audience.

Although, I'm sure they have their moments, like their parents had before them, including the day when Clinton Schutt stepped on the skunk and spurted Billy Hajek.

Hajek had gone on to class stinking like a skunk when the principal went around "sniffing each room" to see where the smell was coming from.

"I was in science class," Hajek recalls, "when he found me."

Carnes took him out of class and got a pair of clean pants from somewhere for him to wear.

"They put the smelly pants behind a bush outside the school." he says.

After school, he had to hold the pants in a white paper bag out a window of the bus until he got to Vanderbilt, where he changed buses. The bag and its contents were then put behind a license plate until he reached his stop.

"It was stinking so bad," he recalls.

He lived a couple of miles north of Vanderbilt, where his father still farms — to the beat of polka music, so I'm told.

Young Hajek went on to become an agriculture teacher at West Columbia and at Industrial High School in Vanderbilt, and also did some farming himself before joining the junior high faculty at Lolita as science teacher nine years ago.

The skunk incident happened when he was in the seventh grade in 1963.

When he got home that day, his folks made him put the stinking pants in the barn.

"May still be there," he says, "for all I know."

School hasn't been stunk up since.

Fiery Sort
(November 16, 1979)

Country school teachers were known for their ability to deal with discipline problems.

They made students work their way out of trouble.

"If you fouled up, you cleaned up the school," Clarence Stauss of Ander says.

There was also the woodpile, where many a boy chopped his way back into good standing with the teacher.

Stauss started school at Ander in 1935.

"I rode a mule to school," he says, "except when the mule had to work in the field. Then I walked."

Stauss recalls cutting wood, and attempting to sneak a smoke at the woodpile. Teacher surprised him one time, and he quickly put the cigarette in his pocket. Says he forgot his pocket was full of kitchen matches.

The teacher really built a fire under him that day.

Smooching Around
(February 26, 1995)

Fire ants make it their home now.

The ant beds dot the two acres that were once a school yard where children played during recess at the old rural Pleasant Grove School, six miles northeast of

Hallettsville between Vsetin and Appelt's Hill.

Two acres were set aside way back in 1881 for the school, which continued up until 1948 after which it was consolidated with the Hallettsville Independent School District.

A typical rural school, one of something like 90 in Lavaca County at one time, now only the cleared grounds remain within the large grove of oak and cedar trees for which the school was named, the schoolhouse having been moved years ago.

I recently visited Pleasant Grove with a number of former students, including 81-year-old Justus Mertz, who started school there in 1920.

Mertz, who still lives in the neighborhood, says he only had to walk about a mile through the pastures to get to the school.

"When I first started," he says, "it was just a one-room school, and then they divided it into two rooms."

He remembers pumping water from a well on the grounds and drinking out of a community cup.

"We weren't poisonous to each other," he says.

He remembers how the boys would climb the many trees around the school "like squirrels," and the hardball games with the little boys playing their games on one side of the school yard and the bigger boys on the other side. He particularly remembers a time when a big boy hit a ball over into the little boys' area.

"They hollered, 'look,' and I did," he recalls. "I got hit right in the eye."

Mertz also remembers the "horse pasture," a fence enclosure adjacent to the school yard in which the children could graze their horses while in class.

Some children were still riding horses to school as late as 1947-48, the last year when Wanda Evans Opela was a "primer," or kindergarten student, with the only other primer that year being Kenneth Orsak.

"He and his brother, R.L., would ride a paint horse to school," she recalls.

The school was back to one room at that time, with

a wood heater, and one teacher, Emily Hornshu, who had been there since 1925.

Little Wanda Evans had to walk about a mile and a half across pastures to get to school, and particularly remembers how difficult it was for her to follow the older kids across Brushy Creek.

"If we went to school," she says, "we walked."

Franklin Hlavac completed his nine years the year before the school closed. He only had to walk a mile to Pleasant Grove but later would walk three miles to Appelt's Hill to catch the bus to Hallettsville.

One of the students who was there the last year, Mae Appelt Rother says there were only three students in her ninth grade class that year, the others being Leonard Woytek and Josephine Zappe Kloesel.

She recalls how the students would go beneath a concrete bridge on a dry creek by the school to eat their lunches.

It was also beneath that bridge where the boys would sometimes "settle their differences."

A little rat terrier dog, "Toby," would accompany her to school and sleep under the teacher's desk, unless he happened to see a squirrel when looking out the door and would run out chasing it.

"Everyone would follow," she recalls.

Mrs. Rother also remembers how they would build log houses out of the wood for the school stove, using the Spanish moss from the trees for the roof and to fill any cracks between the logs.

Some of the boys and girls would take advantage of the seclusion to get in a little smooching.

"Not me, though," she says.

Such schools were a part of a rural life-style that no longer exists as it was for something over 50 years at Pleasant Grove.

A pleasant place for a school.

Playing Hooky
(April 8, 1992)

Bernard Staff remembers once when his entire class decided to play hooky.

It was when the teacher was teaching the big kids — seventh, eighth, ninth, and tenth-graders — at the old Inez School across from the Catholic Church, and it was April Fool's Day.

"It was a kind of common thing," he recalls, "for the older students to skip out on April Fool's."

They had all gathered and started to leave.

"Wait, and I'll go with you," he told them.

Staff was among those reminiscing about experiences at the old school during a reunion at the Garcitas Creek Campground. He taught at Inez and was high school principal there from 1937 to 1941 when it was a three-teacher school.

Retired since 1974, Staff had a long career in education — 43 years altogether — the last 17 years at Mission Valley where he served mostly as superintendent, but also did some teaching.

Staff was raised about four miles south of Telferner on Staff Road and attended the little one-teacher Harmony School in his early years, then rode horseback to high school in Telferner until the 11th year when he came into Victoria to Patti Welder High School where he graduated in 1929.

He later attended Victoria College, then in its beginning years when it was located on the Patti Welder campus, and later went on to San Marcos where he got his degree. He would later get his master's from the University of Houston, but actually began his teaching career when he was only 19 years old.

"In those days," he recalls "you could begin teaching elementary grades after a year of college, and continue your education during the summer. After the second year, you could teach high school."

After eight years, he got his degree, and during that time taught at small one-room schools like Burroughsville, off Lone Tree Road near Victoria.

"I was there five years," he recalls. "Then I went to Casa Blanca for two years, between Wood Hi and Inez."

They were like all the small schools scattered throughout the rural areas at that time, and he remembers days when he had to ride horseback if the weather was bad and he couldn't drive on the roads.

After Inez, he taught a year at Placedo before going into the service, and remembers how they had school six days a week so the students could get out the first part of May and help with the field work since so many of the young men were away at war.

Schools often adjusted schedules for the field work anyway, and he says at times they would only go seven or eight months.

After the war, he was elementary principal at Vanderbilt for a time and then for eight years at Premont in Jim Wells County, before Mission Valley

As for back in Inez, where he had the four grades in one room, Staff says he doesn't know who leaned the most — "me or the kids."

"Me, I guess," he concludes.

When they all decided to play hooky that day, he said there was no way he could corral them — "not 35 of those big kids," as he remembers — so he figured they would just all make a picnic of it.

Fooled around all day and came back.

Burro Bus
(April 21, 1996)

The donkey got tired of being a school bus.

So one day Estelle Lee Pfuhl says it just put its neck down and sat on its haunches, right in the middle of the road near where the Lone Tree School was located two miles north of Petersville.

That is out there on present Farm-to-Market Road 966 off State Highway 111 near Yoakum.

She says the Malek family had the donkey and it was usually loaded down with "no less than six kids riding on its back."

The cars had to go around that day, she says, the donkey just had enough of being overloaded.

Mrs. Pfuhl, who was a Jiral back then, is serving as general chairman of a reunion for nine former rural schools from that general area, including the two-room Lone Tree School which she attended from 1938 to 1945.

"We farmed right next to the school," she recalls. "My dad, Joe Jiral, was a school trustee for many years."

The school closed after 1951 and the old schoolhouse is now a band building at Yoakum High School.

In addition to Lone Tree, the reunion will be for the students from Center, Concrete, Dreyer, Hochheim, Hochheim Prairie, Morris, National Hall, and Prairie View.

Students from Prairie View got the reunions started in 1988 and the other schools have joined in the gathering since, with National Hall and Dreyer coming in this year.

The National Hall School was closed in 1928.

It was 100 years ago to the year that the Lone Tree school was started after an acre of land was deeded by Frank and Tereze Konecny, and Mrs. Pfuhl says Prairie View will be celebrating its centennial at the next reunion.

Lone Tree was a typical two-room school when she attended classes there, the rooms being divided by a folding door so it could be opened into one big room for school and community gatherings. Out back there was a two-car garage for the teachers with a pen around it for the horses and donkeys the students rode to school.

"Sometimes there would be all kinds of kicking and snorting," she recalls, "and the teacher would tell us not to look."

There was a sand table in which the younger children could play and she remembers a boy taking her toy truck.

"It made me mad," she says. "I picked him up and

threw him on the table and buried him."

For that, she had to stand with her nose in a circle on the blackboard and stay in during recess.

"I heard he became a priest," she says.

Three generations of her family attended Lone Tree, including her father before her, her sister Bessie Immenhausen and Bessie's son, Roger.

Mrs. Pfuhl spoke Czech when she started school, except for a few words her mother had taught her at home, how to say "hello, good-bye, please ma'am and thank you ma'am."

"One day I said something in Bohemian to one of the other kids," she recalls, "and the teacher really got on to me about that. She said I had to speak English."

She also remembers the Czech kids teaching the German kids some phrases "that don't need to be repeated."

Like most former students of the rural schools, she wouldn't take for her experiences.

Another thing that Mrs. Pfuhl remembers, how they would have class at times gathered around the wood heater on a cold winter day.

"When state aid came in and the school got commodities," she recalls, "the teacher put a can of beans on the heater and when she punched the can the beans flew out. We even had beans on the ceiling."

They would also warm up water for cocoa.

Share it in an atmosphere of warmth.

Good Memories
(June 15, 1984)

Max Seidenberger says they burned the creek up once at Evergreen School.

He was a student at Evergreen from 1929 to 1936, at the little two-teacher school between Shiner and Moulton near the Henkhaus Community, and at the time they'd go out along the creek at lunch to build a fire and heat their pork sausage, also to sneak cigarettes. This particular time the fire spread to some dry bloodweed along the creek, and Seidenberger said it came close to getting the county bridge. Wasn't so funny at the time, but now they can laugh about burning up the creek.

Seidenberger, now superintendent at Shiner, later taught at Evergreen from 1942 to 1945, also met his wife there, the former Sylvia Tupa. Got to talking to him and Edwin Darilek at the Evergreen School Reunion in Moulton, about some of the games kids used to play around the country schools, and the funny things that would happen from time to time.

Darilek, who was instrumental in organizing the reunion which attracted some 143 families, said he started school there about 1922 and went through eight grades before going on to Shiner. He lived in the Henkhaus Community, where his dad had the cotton gin, later on he and his brother, Laddie, operated the gin there up until it closed in 1973. He says at one time Henkhaus also had a grocery store, blacksmith shop and dance hall.

Evergreen School, which closed in 1951, was on the old Moulton-Shiner road, about a half-mile from where the Sulphur Park swimming pool is now located on the present highway between the two towns in Lavaca County.

They used to play games like red line and scrub baseball at the school, also played something they called jump the creek, according to Seidenberger. The game would start at a narrow spot and move along toward where the creek got wide, wasn't difficult to know when a jumper got eliminated. When the kids got tired of such games, they'd figure out other ways to amuse themselves.

Particularly liked one story that I heard about a girl who got locked in the outhouse, and it wasn't accidental either from what I understand, but she managed to effect an escape that is still considered something of a miracle by those who were there, perpetrators and otherwise. Someone told me she was at the reunion and I would like to have talked to her about that incident, but she slipped away before I could get to her.

Seidenberger was telling about an incident that happened later on, after he had gone to teach at Shiner, about the time Willie Boedecker snorted up a BB in Annie Rasco's class. Seems Willie could put a buckshot in his nose and shoot it clear across the room by holding one nostril, only this time he sucked in too hard before blowing out and the BB went down his windpipe. He said Willie was taken to Wagner Clinic and it looked for awhile like it was going to be necessary to rush him to the hospital in Victoria where they had a gizmo that could retrieve it, until Dr. Frank Wagner came in and looked Willie over good.

"He told Willie to stand on his head and start coughing." Seidenberger recalls.

The BB rolled right out of Willie.

VII

LYE SOAP

Clean Smell
(October 5, 1983)

Monroe Kovar was carrying a box of something that he'd bought in the auction for the Mission Valley Fire Department, showed me what he had in it.

About eight or ten bars of lye soap.

Kovar did the auctioneering, but sold that to himself. Wasn't real sure who made the soap, but said he believes it was one of the Dentlers. For homemade soap, it was pretty smooth looking, some of it that I can remember used to be ugly enough to scare the dirt out of anything.

Soon as I looked in the box, knew what he had in there, got a whiff of it. Always did like the smell of homemade soap, might not be particularly pleasant in the sweet sense, but there is something clean about it.

Kovar gave me a bar to take home, now when the wife starts doing the wash the easy way I can get out my soap and smell of it, think about how mama used to have to do it the hard way. She went through some lye soap in her time, before she got the washing machine and went to something softer.

There was something pleasant about those wash days before we got the washer, especially on a cool morning when the wash kettle would really get to putting up some steam, that's when you could best smell the lye soap. Take a kettle full of overalls, stand over it with one of those plunger things or turn the clothes with a paddle, could get the full benefit of how good it can smell. Remember how dad used to slice the soap off into the hot water with a pocketknife.

Really don't recall just when we quit making lye

soap, presume about the same time we quit butchering hogs, but I was too young to pay all that much attention to such matters at the time. Wish now that I had.

Do remember us cooking soap, and slicing it after it had cooled off in the kettle. It would come out in assorted shapes and sizes when done that way, but that didn't matter when it came to washing with it.

As I recall, mama also used it in the kitchen, least I sure don't recall her using anything else back then. We didn't use it on ourselves, although I've heard of people who did, just the other day a man was telling me that he once dated a girl who washed her hair in lye soap.

Bet she smelled good.

Lots of Grease
(November 4, 1983)

Always enjoy learning when something in this column rings a bell for someone.

We've had numerous folks tell us our comments on lye soap brought forth memories for them, some fond and some not so fond. Really did surprise us how many women said they can remember washing their hair with the stuff, and equally surprised us how many of them still have hair.

If folks were still making lye soap a lot imagine what the government would have to say about it, surely by now it would have killed a rat somewheres. Might have to get a permit to even make it, probably put a warning label on it.

There are still a few people around who do make it, understand from Rudy Laitkep at El Campo that his wife just recently cooked a couple of kettles. He says their friends help out by saving old grease and scrap fat for her to use in the soap.

Remember how we used to save grease like that at home, and how during World War II everybody was asked to turn in what they didn't use, they supposedly made some sort of explosive out of it. Have always wondered about that, if it might not have been more a ploy to get people involved in the war effort than anything else. One thing about it, we always had plenty of old grease to give.

The health officials would gasp in horror today if they had to eat food the way we did, lots of grease and more salt than you could shake a stick at, not to mention all the milk, the eggs, and so much starch you'd get a stiff collar just by eating dinner. Know a lot of folks who used to eat like that, some of them are in their 80s and 90s now, guess they were just too tough for all that food to kill.

One thing about it, none of that food had any preservatives in it to speak of, other than for the salt and maybe a little saltpetre or something like that in the meat, seemed to me like it was all pretty wholesome.

Laitkep says his wife does something else that folks don't do a lot anymore, she catches rainwater in barrels for washing clothes. We used to do it for that and for drinking, and there is just nothing better for washing clothes, and it wasn't bad drinking either.

Rainwater has a different taste to it than most of us are accustomed to now, of course with all the chemicals in the air it might not be fit to drink at all. Notice it's beginning to rain outside as I'm writing this, probably wouldn't take long to find out.

Might be good to wash down a TV dinner.

Floating Soap
(September 4, 1984)

Heard a neighbor once describe another neighbor's wife as being ugly as homemade soap.

That's ugly.

I can remember the woman, and she certainly wasn't

the Ivory girl, would say she was a bit on the coarse side, not that she wasn't a good woman. We're strictly talking looks here, and soaps. Just happened to be reading something that reminded me of something we wrote last October about lye soap, and a letter that we received from Mrs. R.H. Matson.

Mrs. Matson had told us how she learned the art of soap making from her mother-in-law, in the days of the Ivory soap commercials on the radio — "99 and 44/100 percent pure and it floats." She said her homemade soap would also float, just like the Ivory. A floating soap was something to be rather proud of, even though Mrs. Matson said she didn't know exactly what she did to get her's to do it.

Hadn't thought much about it since, but the other day while reading some old columns by Ernie Pyle, written before he became so famous as a correspondent during World War II, I came across one he wrote after visiting Cincinnati, which some friends had told him was famous for "music, stories, and soap." Ernie said since he didn't understand classical music, or stories either, that it left him nothing to write about except soap.

He set out to look into Cincinnati's leading industry, visiting the factory of Procter & Gamble, producers of about 40 percent of America's soap at the time, and guess what he asked first, right off the bat.

"What makes Ivory soap float?"

Pyle said he had to ask three people before he found one who knew, that Ivory soap floated because it was whipped and beaten much longer than other soaps of that time, and that it was full of tiny air cells.

"As far as I could learn," he said. "This extra whipping doesn't do the soap any good — or any harm either; just makes it float."

He said while cooking it looked exactly like the brown soap his mother used to make out of cracklings and lye in a black kettle over an outside fire, but when processed became beautiful cakes with a come hither smell.

Pyle couldn't resist the temptation to ask if they put dead horses in it, and said he was frankly told by the soap people they wouldn't be surprised if an occasional horse did stray into the tallow, but he said the main staple in the company's soaps was coconut oil, which had replaced whale oil since whales were becoming extinct.

Don't know if I should have mentioned what the neighbor said about that other neighbor's wife, repeating that sort of thing could get a boy's mouth washed out with soap.

Oh, well, make it Ivory.

Hair Raising
(March 4, 1986)

Folks who use lye soap to wash their hair say it's good for the scalp.

My wife thinks I'm out of my head.

Told her it didn't matter, that I was going to try it anyway, and I did, with a fresh bar I got Sunday at the Settler's Day from Dan and Joyce Dentler of Mission Valley. They had a soap making exhibit that attracted a lot of attention at the event sponsored by the Victoria County Senior Citizens, and Mrs. Dentler was telling me she uses it sometimes on her hair. Looked to me like she has pretty good hair, so I figured it might work for me.

"You didn't," the wife commented when I came out of the bathroom with a wet head."

"I sure did," I said, "and it feels good."

I've been looking for something for years that will give my hair some body and make my scalp quit itching, and Mrs. Dentler said folks sometimes ask them for the soap just to wash their hair.

"We have an old German friend at Blanco who says his head hasn't bothered him since he started using it," she said.

Hope that old German knows what he's talking

about.

The Dentlers sure make some pretty homemade soap, and it makes a nice lather. Might even try it on my whiskers sometimes if it works on my head, since I certainly could use a little body in that respect. They put a little Pine Sol in their soap, which gives it a nice smell, although I've always liked the smell of just plain old homemade soap. Monroe Kovar gave me a bar of Dentler soap a couple of years ago when he did an auction at the Mission Valley Fire Department's chili cook-off, and I take a smell of it every so often just for the smell of it. Kind of reminds me of back when I was a kid and we used to make soap at home, although our soap was a little different since we made it from cracklings. It's not near as pretty as the soap made from pure fat, but we had to get the lard out first or we wouldn't have had anything to cook with. That soap was brown and rather coarse looking, and that's why folks used to say that something unattractive was ugly as homemade soap.

The Dentler's soap is almost as pretty as the store bought kind.

Mrs. Dentler says she saves all kinds of fat to make their soap, even chicken skin.

Hope I don't start growing any feathers.

"We have another friend in Floresville who butchers fed cattle," she says, "and he gives us four or five gallons of fat at a time."

The soap isn't all that hard to make and they were giving out some recipes. You put about 20 pounds of unrendered and coarsely ground or finely cut tallow in a wash pot, add two gallons of water and four cans of lye, stir and mix well. Let that stand about five minutes before applying the heat, and after it comes to a boil let it roll for about five minutes before removing from the heat. Then slowly add a gallon of water to which a cup of Pine Sol and quarter-pound of Borax has been added, and stir continually until the soap begins to thicken. You then pour it into molds and let it cool overnight, then cut it into bars.

There's also "stir soap" that can be made on the

kitchen stove in about 45 minutes using five pounds of grease, seven cups of water, and a can of lye.

The Dentlers make quite a bit of soap, and what they don't use they give to Lutheran World Relief, which sends it to foreign countries where soap isn't taken for granted like it is in this country. In fact, it's considered quite a luxury in some places. From pictures I've seen on television, it would appear to me some of those folks could really use a bar of lye soap

It did make my scalp feel real good, but I wish now that I'd asked Mrs. Dentler a little more about that old German friend at Blanco. Would kind of like to know what his head looks like.

Make sure he still has his hair.

Worrying Worse
(March 14, 1986)

Emma Chubb says not to worry about using the lye soap on my hair.

"It will not hurt the hair or head," she says. "I had long light brown hair my mother washed with lye soap they made themselves until we left the farm."

Mrs. Chubb says she had heavy hair until her daughter cut it off the year before because it's hard for her to take care of now.

"I am 94 years old," she says. "Will be 95 on Aug. 12."

Remember visiting several years ago with Mrs. Chubb, who was married to the artist and painter Tom Pace in 1912 when he got the job of painting the new town of Austwell, which was being developed by Preston R. Austin and associates. Pace also painted some murals during that time, including one that was at Bluhm's Drug Store many years and has since been displayed at the Flores Grocery. We had talked about old times then, but don't remember if we got on the subject of lye soap.

The mere mention of lye soap brings back memories

for many of us, and I guess the name gets youngsters curious about it, know it seemed like all ages were taking an interest in the exhibit that Dan and Joyce Dentler had at the Settler's Day where they gave me a bar to wash my hair with. It has made my hair feel good so far, and I'm glad to hear from Mrs. Chubb that it's not going to fall out.

She says her older sister married a barber who told them never to use shampoo, but to use lye soap instead, and she says they grew long and heavy hair. She says after the family left the farm they switched to Oxydol, which she continues to use.

"I rinse my hair with cider vinegar," she says. "Added to the last rinse water."

Since I'm on the subject of cleanliness, in a round about way, might mention something that Elizabeth Stockbauer told me at the Settlers' Day, about the Japanese rice farmers at DaCosta in the early 1900s. She remembers her father, Edmund Nitschmann, talking about when the Japanese were there and how they used to bathe in the irrigation canals. They would line up naked, each with their hands on the shoulders of the ones in front, and then they'd all trot off to the canal and jump in.

Mrs. Stockbauer's grandfather, Josef Nitschmann, was instrumental in the development of DaCosta.

The bathing habits of the Japanese were evidently a constant source of amazement to the locals. The late Paul Freier, in his historical writings bout Calhoun County, mentioned how the Japanese had requested special tubs while staying at the Lavaca Hotel. They wanted the round, deep wooden tubs they were accustomed to bathing in at home. Some folks thought it had religious significance, but actually it was just the way they liked to get clean. Would be curious to know what they used to wash their hair.

One thing I know that's good for hair is rainwater, and I've heard that beer makes a good rinse, also I've heard something about using the whites of raw eggs. I even read somewhere that mayonnaise is good for dry hair, and onion juice is supposed to be good for bald spots. The way I see it, if I didn't have the hair I wouldn't have the worry.

Have always heard worrying can make your hair fall out.

VIII

SATURDAY BATHS

Needed, or Not
(September 13, 1985)

A lady who wouldn't give her name called to ask something this week that I'd really never thought much about before.

Wanted to know how the old-timers got by without taking more baths than they did.

I suppose they got used to each other.

It wasn't that they were dirty people necessarily, the opportunity just didn't always exist to bathe often, and back then some folks didn't think it was healthy to take a lot of baths to begin with, even when I was a kid it was commonly held that bathing too often would make a person weak. Come to think of it, the real scrubbed people did seem to be weaker than the others, but I doubt if bathing had a lot to do with it. I think that was just a belief that made it more bearable to go without, but then again I have seen some people who weren't particularly fond of bathing who seemed awfully healthy to me.

Now I think the lady was talking about further back than that, but bathing as most of us practice it now wasn't all that widespread even when I was little, especially out in the country where the Saturday night

bath was still a ritual practiced in most rural homes. We had one of those galvanized No. 3 tubs up until I was in high school, then we got a regular bathtub like now, except there wasn't any hot water and we still had to heat it on the stove. It was a lot of trouble taking a bath, especially if you didn't need one and it was generally considered that once a week was enough, except the women liked to sponge off once in awhile for beauty's sake. Sponge baths, that's what they called them.

The footbath was also popular, but I think that was more for tired feet than cleanliness. As long as a person was clean on Sunday morning for church, the rest of the week didn't matter all that much because even if you did bathe you'd just get dirty all over again. I remember when we were working in the field during maize harvest or other dirty work, then sometimes the men would shower off under the windmill or maybe set up a tub outside, course that was during the summer when you could do that. In the winter, we just went from one Saturday until the next.

I think we really had it pretty good, when you consider how it must have been back before that, imagine what it was like in a covered wagon, or a log cabin, or worse yet for months on the ocean in one of those old immigrant ships. Those folks had to get a little rank at times, but I'll bet when they did get to bathe they appreciated it, now folks think it's something to do every time they feel a little sweaty, like when the air conditioning isn't working right.

Course the city folks had it a little better than the country folks, at least after running water came along. In Victoria, from best I can tell, that was about 1884 when a pumping station was built on the Guadalupe River and water was piped directly into homes. I would think bathing became a lot more popular after that.

Not to mention healthy.

IX

WASH DAYS

An Occasion
(October 13, 1983)

Mrs. R.H. Matson says our recent comments on lye soap sure brought back memories for her.

"Carrying water, chopping wood, deciding which side of the clothesline to make the fire so that smoke wouldn't ruin the clean clothes — and the soap," she says.

Also reminded her of the old irons that were heated on a smoky coal oil stove.

"By the time you got them clean enough to use, they were almost cold again," she recalls.

She says young 'uns sure have it hard today, remembering to remove their permanent press from the dryer so it won't wrinkle.

Sometimes wonder myself if they would believe it even if they saw it, wouldn't even seem like the same world to them. It was hard work, just keeping the family's clothes halfway decent. I can remember quite well those wash days, watching my mama bent over a rubbing board, most women don't work as hard in a month as she did on one wash day.

Mrs. Matson said her first knowledge of the art of soap making came from her mother-in-law, Mrs. A.C. Matson. She said those were the days of the Ivory soap commercial on the radio — "99 and 44/100 percent pure and it floats" — but they didn't have anything on her, least not about the floating part.

She recalls that both her soap and her mother-in-law's would get clothes clean and smelling like a fresh morning breeze, but that her soap had that added advantage, it would float, just as sure as the Ivory would.

"I tell you, Mrs. Matson all but turned green with envy," she recalls, but says to this day she doesn't know what she did to make it float.

Walk down the soap and detergent row in a supermarket today, kind of hard to believe there was ever a time when just the fact that a soap would float could be of so much significance, now they have them doing just about everything but the washing itself.

They will brighten, lighten and bring out the color, make clothes soft and fluffy, and all you have to do is pour a little bit in the washing machine, set the dial to wherever you want it, then watch your favorite soap opera on the television, between detergent commercials.

There's just not much left to washing anymore, somehow I think there was more fun to it back when there was more work to it, seemed much more a part of life back then, not just another one of the little agitating everyday chores that seem to get in the way of everything else. Least I always thought wash day was something of an occasion, even though as best I can remember our soap didn't float.

Not for long anyway.

Strong Winds
(November 20, 1992)

Nothing could make Mama run faster than a strong wind.

When she had clothes on the line.

Strong winds could mean one of two things out in

West Texas — either a dust storm was blowing in or we were having a blue norther — and with either one a woman didn't want to have clothes hanging.

A whole line of clothes frozen stiff wasn't any fun to have to thaw out later in the house, and worse yet was when a dust storm came and the wash would get all dirty again.

MAMA! WE'RE PLUMB OUT OF BLUING!

—THEN HOW IN THE WORLD ARE WE GOING TO GET OUT THIS BIG WASHING?

A RED ANT STUNG ME! WHERE'S THE BLUING?

WASHDAY BRIGHTENER — IT WASN'T HAWKED ON TV, BUT GROCERY STORES OVER THE NATION HAD BOTTLES OF BLUING ON SHELVES TO MAKE WASHDAYS BRIGHTER

STICKS STAHALA

Don't know just what got me to thinking about wash days and clothes hanging on the line, but things have sure changed since then.

It's like living in Paradise on wash days today.

I remember well back to the time when Mama did all her washing out in the yard with the heavy work clothes in a big iron kettle — the wash pot — and we had one of those plunger things with a handle to make the clothes come clean.

There was also a wooden paddle to turn the heavy wash and carry it to the rinse, and Dad would help when he wasn't working in the field.

Youngsters today would find it hard to believe, what it took just to do the weekly washing, and it was a full day's work in between Mama making dinner.

One modern convenience she did have at the time was a hand wringer between two tubs, one filled with rinse water and as I recall, the other with the bluing water.

I imagine some younger women today have never even heard of bluing.

I always thought the blue water was pretty, sorta like I expected the ocean to be, and it amazed me that something so blue could get clothes to look fresher and brighter.

It was all done out in the yard, weather permitting, and it didn't matter how hot or how cold unless it was freezing and the clothes couldn't be hung on the line.

In the summers, my Mama would be out there sweating in a thin cotton dress with no bra on, which I mention only because the girls of the 60s and 70s just thought they were doing something new when they started going without, but then Mama wouldn't have ever been caught in public without one.

It was purely for survival on a hot wash day.

That was all before we got the wringer washing machine, just after World War II as I recall, and Mama was about the happiest woman I ever saw when it arrived.

Don't remember when the automatic washer came some years later, but it could not have been half the thrill of the day she got the old wringer. It brought a big change to wash day.

This was also all before wash-and-wear clothes, of course, and I might add, disposable diapers, although I don't remember back to when Mama was washing diapers.

That could have been done inside in a small tub, because I'm sure the diapers couldn't wait for a wash day to be washed.

If young women today had to go through that, they would think they had done died and gone to the wrong place.

There wasn't much fun to wash days that I remember, except I always did like the smell of the lye soap bubbling up in the wash pot and the pretty color of the bluing water, and the smell of clean sheets and shirts just off the line which never smell so good otherwise.

I also got a kick out of seeing Mama run when there was a wind coming and she had clothes on the line, because in those days one never saw women run like we do now. I wouldn't even think of trying to keep up with her.

Even when she was carrying a full load.

Battling Block
(November 25, 1992)

Euner Johnson tells me that I left out a step when writing about the old-time wash days.

The battling block.

I don't recall us ever having one, but then, as I mentioned, we had a plunger to get the dirt out of the heavy clothes, which I suppose was a pretty modern gadget at some point in time.

It was something that looked like a big plumber's

friend, the kind that is used in the bathroom, only the bottom part was made of metal and somehow let the water go through so the clothes could be plunged clean.

The battling block, as Mrs. Johnson explains, was used between the rinse water and the wash pot and was usually just an old stump where one could beat out the water and heavy dirt.

"A natural stump was okay," she says, "and, if not, you could put one in."

She said that's the way they did it in Mississippi, at least.

Enjoyed visiting with her for awhile at the Victoria Symphony's Christmas in November arts and crafts show where Emily Buckert and I had set up to autograph our books, and Mrs. Johnson came by with the DeDear sisters, Doris Kelso and Lena Stark, all from down around Austwell and Tivoli.

Mrs. Johnson's late husband, Frank, was manager of Aransas Wildlife Refuge and I particularly remember visiting with him once right after I had started Henry's Journal in 1979, and it just happened to be around the time when the bow hunters were there.

Some of the stories about the bow hunters on the refuge have become legend, and one I particularly remember had to do with an old boy and his wife who had a little marital trouble during the hunt.

Don't recall if it started out that way or just ended with a fight, but from what I recall the hunter had staked their tent to his truck when the wind had come up during the night.

The next morning, he got ready to go hunting and jumped in the truck and was dragging tent, wife and all along behind him.

Way Johnson described it, that was one mad woman.

Good thing the woman wasn't near a battling block or she might have used the clothes paddle on her husband, since some of the witnesses to the incident said she was still beating on him when they left for home.

I just happened to remember the story while talking

with Mrs. Johnson.

Want to mention a couple of other folks that came by the booth last weekend, like Pat Pursel, who is a cook with the Coast Guard at Port O'Connor and gave us a new way to make S.O.S., which my wife does make occasionally just to remind me of my days in the Air Force when we met.

That's chipped beef on toast usually, but Pursel suggested trying sausage sometimes instead, with maybe a bit of cut up bacon.

He happens to be from my old country out around San Angelo.

I was going to mention Geneva MacGaffick of Hallettsville and her fancy outhouse, but guess that will wait for another time since I'm about out of space.

Mrs. Johnson had mentioned something else, like how after the clothes were finally washed the kids could play in the rinse water.

It was a lot like having a hot tub.

Not So Blue
(November 17, 1995)

Memories of wash days are not so blue for Henri Mae Mertz of El Campo.

Unlike today, when washing is such an easy routine in most homes — "sort the clothes, put in washer, add detergent, select type of wash, and press 'on' button, and you're in business," as she notes — it was a different story back 60 years ago in rural America.

"Then my family, Mom, Dad and five kids lived on a farm seven miles northwest of Yoakum in the Lone Tree School area," she says. "Our wash day was usually on a Friday morning, so everything would be clean for the weekend, in case company would come on Sunday.

"First, we filled the iron kettle with water carried by bucketfuls from the cistern. Kindling had to be gathered for the fire we built under the kettle.

"We sorted the clothes, soaked the whites in cold water to help loosen the dirt. We three older girls took turns rubbing the clothes on a rubbing board, then put them in the kettle to boil for about 15 minutes.

"We'd wring out most of the soapy water, then rinse in two tubs, the last one being the 'blue rinse.'"

Sometimes they would accidentally overdo the bluing.

"Which didn't set too well with Mom," she recalls

"All during this time, we had to keep the fire going under the kettle for the other batch of clothes," she adds. "This chore usually fell to our brother Mark.

"He was a real cutup and kept us in stitches. In the winter time, he loved to 'snitch' sausage out of the smokehouse and roast it over the hot coals.

"It did taste good."

"Finally, it was time to hang out the wash," she says. "The sun and wind were our 'dryer' and the clothes certainly had a good, clean, fresh smell that we still remember."

They usually did the laundry under shady chinaberry trees, but in cold weather moved to "the south side of the smokehouse."

Which, I presume, made it even more convenient for brother Mark.

At any rate, she says this routine continued until the late 1930s when the family got a manually-operated washer with a wringer.

"We thought we were in high cotton," she recalls.

"Even if wash days were a lot of work," she says. "I enjoyed them. At least we didn't have to go to the cotton patch."

I doubt if youngsters today would feel the same way about wash days, but then they have never experienced the cotton patch either and, as she points out, wash days did have their moments.

Once when I was sent to a neighbor's house with a message — another kid chore — the woman was hanging wash and I got to chatting with her husband on their back porch. I had my BB gun with me, and we were talking about it as his wife was bending over a basket of wet clothes.

"Bet you can't hit that," he said.

That woman almost jumped over the clothes line.

X

BUTCHER CLUBS

Once Popular
(September 11, 1980)

Almost every community had one.

"To me, it was democracy in action," says Edwin Darilek, who belonged to one.

He was speaking of the meat clubs that were once popular throughout the state, the means by which many families had fresh meat on the table each week, at least for a day or two.

Not many of the clubs are still in existence, but we did run across one over in the Henkhaus Community of Lavaca County, between Moulton and Shiner.

Darilek was a member of that club for about 20 years, and he introduced me to the man who serves as its meat cutter now, Frank W. Wagner. His dad, Charles F. Wagner, was a member of the old Wagner meat club, which eventually combined with the neighboring Henkhaus club.

"There's been a meat club in the community for 75 or 80 years now," Wagner says, noting that he himself has participated in one for 52 years.

The club only has eight members, compared to the 24 that used to be considered ideal, in the days when a calf was butchered every week, hogs in the winter. Now they butcher every three weeks, many of the members having their calves killed and dressed at a slaughterhouse, then bringing the dressed carcass to Gus's Place near Moulton where the meat is divided up.

In the old days, each member butchered his own calf, usually getting started about 4 a.m. in the cool of the morning. After the meat was divided up, members would take it home, where the wife would usually have to cook up most of it so that it would keep. Some might be put in the well, where it would stay fresh for a day or two.

The way a club works, each member pledges a calf, then the butchering order is established by drawing numbers. A limit is set on the dressed weight, and any member having a calf that goes over that must donate the difference to the club. If it goes under, they pay the difference, based on a price per pound agreed to at the beginning.

During the course of a year, members might get more than their share, or less, which is all settled up at the end. Records are kept by a bookkeeper, like George Technik.

Wagner says each member gets a different cut of calf at each butchering.

"That way they end up with a whole calf," he points out.

He says the cutter used to get four bits each time for his work, the bookkeeper half of that.

"Now I get $1.50," he says. "The bookkeeper gets a dollar."

In addition to Wagner and Technik, other members of the club are Johnnie Dierschke, Elo Seifert, Albert Krejci, Alvin Meyer, Oscar Marburger and Johnny Zissa.

The meat clubs were just one of many ways rural neighbors used to work together for the common good.

It's always nice to find a bunch of neighbors who still enjoy working together. Sometimes we forget that most of our rural communities got started that way to begin with.

There wouldn't be a Henkhaus Community or a meat club if it hadn't been that way.

Last in Lavaca
(January 30, 1994)

Melvin Christen can remember carrying meat home as a boy on horseback.

When his dad, Joe, belonged to a meat club in Moravia, and young Christen would carry their share home in a flour sack tied to the horn of his saddle.

"With a picksack under it," he recalls.

Christen is now 75 years old and belongs to the last meat club in Lavaca County and possibly all of South Texas, even the state.

Meat clubs began to fade out years ago with the coming of electricity and refrigerators to rural Texas, and also the locker plants after World War II that made it possible for farm families to keep a supply of fresh meat available, but otherwise the meat clubs were often the way for a family to have fresh beef on a regular basis.

Some did continue to operate in Lavaca County and the only existing one now meets every third Friday at Blase's Place, about five miles west of Hallettsville on U.S. Highway 90A, and it consists of 12 members having once belonged to other clubs in the county.

"This was originally the old Worthing Club," explains Alfonse Steffek, the club's bookkeeper and meat cutter who joined the original club some 45 years ago.

"Back then we butchered every week," he says.

Christen and his son-in-law, Franklin Neubauer, share a membership, and in addition to them and Steffek, members include Jim Vanek, Paul Janak, Leroy Boedecker, Dennis Hildebrandt, Hilbert Bludau, Leo Bludau, Adolph Opella, Johnnie Dierschke, Ignac Krejci and Don Gathier.

Every three weeks they butcher a calf that dresses out from 300 to 350 pounds, giving each member about 25 to 30 pounds of fresh meat, and the carcass is divided in a way that over a 36-week period each member receives what would amount to a whole calf.

Each member furnishes a calf when it comes his time to do so, and the one that furnishes the calf gets to "do the sawing" and also gets to keep, in addition to his share of meat, such things as the tongue, liver, heart, kidneys, leg bones, brains, and the tail bone.

While calves were generally butchered on the farm in

the old days, they are now taken to Glen's Meat Market in Hallettsville and the club only has to handle the carcass itself.

Some members still feed their own calves, but others let Glen Dolezal buy a calf for them.

"He knows what the club needs," Neubauer points out. "It's about 50-50 now."

At the end of each full butchering cycle, it is tallied up how much meat each member contributed and received, and then they either pay or get paid for the difference at $1.20 a pound.

That way everybody comes out even.

Members say they like the fresh meat because it has a better flavor than that which has already been chilled and to them it is worth the trouble of dividing a calf every three weeks.

There is also the enjoyment of just getting together.

Christen, who has belonged to a number of different clubs over the years, says that he can remember when they started butchering at 2 a.m. in the cool of the morning.

"We would be through by five and have fresh beef for breakfast," he says.

It was more sanitary to butcher at night when there were no flies around.

Took a little more doing in the old days.

XI

HOG KILLING

Family Affair
(January 12, 1992)

Granddaughter Connie wanted to know where I was going.

"To a hog killing," I answered.

"Gross," she said.

Don't guess she's ever been any closer to a hog than at the stock show or maybe when she's had bacon for breakfast, and I doubt if she would have fully appreciated what was happening at Eldor Buehring's place in the Oak Grove Community about 2½ miles west of Witting, where members of three generations of the family had gathered for just one of a number of butcher days they have each winter.

It's a family affair and something you don't see much anymore, especially where they pretty well do the butchering like it was done in the old days, from shooting the hog and scraping it to cutting the meat and stuffing sausage and even rendering lard. But, even they don't do it all the old way, like they no longer cure the hams and bacon at home — the hams become roasts and the bacon goes to town to be cured. They do smoke the sausage and otherwise it's all pretty much the way I remember hog killings.

What's great about it, the younger generation is given an opportunity to learn some of the skills required, starting with the shooting of the hog, a skill now shared by Michael Chaloupka and his grandfather, Eldor, who used to reserve that duty for himself. It's not always easy to dispatch a hog properly.

Some of the other young helpers on the Saturday when I was there included Amanda Koch, 11, who has been helping since she was seven or so with cutting and grinding the meat; Jason Olsovsky, 9, who was doing some of the same; and Jeremy Buehring, 11, who had the job of driving the tractor to bring the hog up after it was shot. They do that with a wooden sled on a round bale mover, not so different from when we used to drag the hog up on a sled for scraping.

Buehring says when he was a kid growing up in Karnes County that they used to drag the hog up behind a mule.

"We'd use one of the gentler mules, one that wouldn't spook if he saw the hog behind him," he recalls. "Dad would butcher two hogs and one old cow that he had fattened."

Back in those days it was all done from scratch at home, and he recalls how his dad would fry the ribs and put them down in lard to keep for when they would need the meat at cotton picking time, and he also made dried beef. Everything was salted down or smoked, and the dry pork sausage could later be put down in the larder for keeping well into the summer.

They didn't have any conveniences, like the electric sausage grinder they were using last Saturday, but otherwise it was much the same and everybody pitched in and had their particular chores to do.

Buehring said the way they got started doing it all together was when he decided to raise and give each of his six children a hog for Christmas.

"They buy the pigs now," he says, "but I raise them since I have the feed and a place to keep them."

Most of the children live where they couldn't keep hogs themselves, and this year a granddaughter, Mrs.

Joe "Melissa" Chapman-Ramirez of Crosby, was also included, and it was her hog that was among the two they were butchering when I was there.

The Buehring children include Mrs. Edward "Allyne" Chapman, Mrs. Ernest "Helen" Chaloupka Jr., Mrs. Paul "Marilyn" Hanslik, Mrs. John "Kathy" Koch, Mrs. Sylvin "Loretta" Olsovsky, and Robert Buehring.

The cooking on butchering days is done by Mrs. Buehring, who was being assisted by daughter Loretta, and I'm told she also makes it her job to make sure the casings are well washed for the sausage, a chore not near as bad as it was in the old days when they came right from the hog itself.

One thing I probably ought to mention, before going to the smokehouse with this, and that is the Buehring family says for a successful hog killing there is something you sure need.

Plenty of good polka music.

Seasoning Ceremony
(April 18, 1989)

Gene Warzecha recalls how his daddy used to check the sausage to make sure the seasoning was right.

"He would fry one little patty," he says. "It was like a ceremony."

Warzecha said everybody would get a little taste, but that his dad was always the final judge when it came to seasoning the sausage.

We got to talking about sausage making and hog killing during the Braggin' Rights Sausage Contest at the Yorktown Springfest, where Warzecha was one of the judges. They didn't have a lot of teams for the first year, but there was a variety of sausage and the big winner turned out to be Wilburn Arndt, an experienced sausage maker from Lindenau.

Arndt won first place in the dry, smoked and cooked divisions.

He got started making country sausage after the Korean War when some of the stores wanted it, like Albert Kuester's in Lindenau, or Osterloh's in Cuero and Wehman's. He was selling to 12 or 13 stores, but says now he just does custom work. He also buys his pork, where back in the beginning he did everything the old way.

"I started butchering under a tree," he says, "and used everything the hog had."

That's also about the way it was when Warzecha was at home.

His dad was Eddie, and mama is Lillian, and he describes them as "dream parents."

"I didn't know it back then," he says, "but they let me be myself, be independent."

"Dad always said, 'We got good kids,'" Warzecha recalls. "It always sounded good to me even if it wasn't always true."

Warzecha is one of any number of young men who grew up around Yorktown who have in the past decade or so returned home to raise their families. He had been in San Antonio where he still has two sisters living, but said in 1980 that he was selling real estate and the market had gone bad, his dad was getting ill, and he and his wife, Elaine, also wanted to get their kids to a small town.

When he was a boy, Warzecha said his family always killed hogs — on up to about 1966 — and customarily killed a hog or a calf on the same day.

"Boy, that was a work day," he recalls.

It was also always a cold day, and he particularly recalls how cold their hands would get while mixing the sausage. Then, sometimes they'd have to mix it again, if the seasoning wasn't right.

"Then we'd stuff it," he says.

Next came smoking the sausage, usually three times over a period of three days, and that was his job and one he always liked.

Not a bad thing to be doing on a cold winter day.

Smell of Smoke
(December 20, 1994)

The whole neighborhood would smell good.

Sort of like it does sometimes now on the north side

of town in Otto Bleier's neighborhood when he has sausage smoking, or out at Edgar Mueller's at Kemper City, but it's never like it was back when just about everybody in the country and a lot of folks in town had smokehouses.

Get a really good cold spell that looked like it might linger for awhile, and it would be butchering time and the smoke would be everywhere, not just around a house here and there.

The people I know mostly smoke sausage now, usually a mixture of pork and deer meat, but back then, of course, smokehouses would be filled with pure pork sausage, bacon and hams, and maybe a crock in the corner with salted jowl and pigs feet — back when we did the whole hog.

I went out to visit with Mueller for awhile Saturday to talk sausage, since he's been around sausage making out there on the home place for nearly 75 years, and makes a really good dry sausage.

It takes a particular skill to make dry sausage that is dry and yet soft enough to chew, and he uses about two-thirds deer meat to a third of pork, the latter being half pork fat and half Boston butt.

"It needs a little fat or it gets too dry," he points out.

While he uses the same mixture for regular smoked sausage with deer meat, Mueller says pure pork is still best for good "cooking sausage."

Mueller never uses deer shank in his sausage.

"It's too tough," he says, "and, if by accident, you get a little musk in it, you ruin the taste."

This has been a tough fall for sausage making, since we haven't had any prolonged cold weather, and drying sausage can ruin when the weather gets too hot and humid.

Mueller says sometimes the only way to save it is to put it in a cooler for awhile, or one can dry it out in a frost-free refrigerator if they have room to lay it out.

He gives his sausage two good smokings of four to five hours, then normally lets it dry for three weeks in the smokehouse.

Old-timers had to really watch the weather when it came to butchering, and there have been some mild falls before, like Mueller was recalling there were late blooms on cotton in the fields one Christmas in the early 1930s.

With bacon and hams, they used a whole lot of salt in curing the meat, and they would remove the bone from the ham so it wouldn't spoil as easily.

Before frying some of the salted bacon, they would parboil it, he recalls.

They would also put sausage and bacon down in lard, and salt down the leg, neck and backbones, and maybe fresh cook the feet, tongue and sometimes the ears with bay leaf and then pack it in a bowl of vinegar with sliced onions to jell overnight.

"Mother would clean the stomach and put head cheese in it," he says, "and it would be smoked with the sausage."

I'm reminded of what my dad always said, when we were butchering a hog.

Save everything but the squeal.

XII

MEAT MARKETS

Valuable Lesson
(April 22, 1980)

A young man in the early 1920s who wanted a dollar or two in his pocket when he needed it knew what he had to do to get it.

Find himself a steady job.

A.M. Buckert had been raised as a farmer since the day he was born on the bank of the Guadalupe River south of Victoria during a flood. His father, Henry, was a farmer, as was his grandpa Louis who had settled on the river about 1860.

Farmers always seemed to have plenty to eat, but money was hard to come by.

Buckert figured if he was ever going to have any that he'd better get himself a job, so he went looking.

That's how he ended up in a meat market at 710 E. Juan Linn which he managed for about 14 years until he purchased it in 1935 and operated it on his own up until 1941.

He first worked there for the Simon brothers, Clarence, E.J. and Leonard, who had a large market at 504 S. Main and operated the Juan Linn location as a branch.

"I'm so green that if you stick me in the ground I'll

grow," Buckert told his new boss, "but I'm willing to learn."

After about a week in training, he was put in charge of the market, at $50 a month which he considered a pretty good wage. Increases didn't come fast, but they did come and when their first child was born there was a note with his check that it was being increased five dollars owing to the increase in the family.

The meat market was adjacent to the Sitterle family's old Round House Trading Co., where at the time a grocery store was being operated by Elmer Bisset and Will Ed Marberry. It changed hands a couple of times during the years Buckert was next door.

Buckert has a picture of his market taken by a "hobo" which shows him behind the counter. There are some smoked meats hanging from a rack, and there's a big walk-in cooler behind him where the fresh meat was kept cold with 100-pound blocks of ice.

"Better cuts of meat sold for around 20 cents a pound for ten years or more," Buckert says. "Bacon was six cents a pound during the Depression and we couldn't get rid of it."

After the Buckert boys, Marvin and Albert Jr., were old enough they helped their parents with deliveries.

Marvin recalls getting 50 cents a week, but it also meant he could make more deliveries. He's still not sure just how well he came out on the deal.

It was good training for the day when the boys would go out looking for a job on their own.

A young man who knows what it takes to earn a dollar has some idea of the value of one, or vice versa.

They know the meaning of a steady job.

Like A.M. Buckert did when he came off the farm looking for one.

One that lasted until he was ready to retire and do a little farming.

Cattle Town
(November 4, 1993)

Victoria was quite a cowtown when J.M. Fimbel was growing up at Cameron and North streets in Victoria.

That was the edge of town at the time, in the teens and 20s, and there wasn't much else north or east. His dad had four blocks leased toward the boulevard and Fimbel used to have to get up and herd the milk cows out to graze each morning before going to school.

Most all of that was open land and one could find cows grazing there and at just about any other open spot around town. Out behind where Patti Welder Intermediate School is now, before it was built as a high school, the Welder Ranch used to have some cattle pens, and the cowboys would bed down herds of steers there when they were driving them from Blue Mott north of town to Green Lake south of town. Could hear them bellowing all over town when the wind was right.

Fimbel says he particularly remembers an old cook named Nick that used to work the Welder chuck wagon, and what good bread he made.

There were other pens in the vicinity where Groce-Wearden (Scrivner) has its warehouses now, there on the railroad where thousands upon thousands of cattle were shipped out over the years, where countless others got dipped for ticks.

Fimbel's daddy, Edwin, was a cattle buyer and bought a lot of cattle for Ed Simon, who had a two-story butcher house behind St. Mary's Church with a long meat shed out back, another market on Juan Linn near the Round House Grocery, and a feedlot and slaughterhouse on the south edge of town. Fimbel says he can still hear the sounds of the old motor running as sausage was being ground in the shed behind St. Mary's. Simon was Fimbel's uncle.

Fimbel says when he was maybe 10 to 12 years old he used to help his dad drive cattle in from the country, over the wood-bottomed bridge on the Guadalupe River, one of those old bridges that made all kinds of racket when something was crossing it. Some horses and mules would hardly go over it, and cattle didn't like it either.

"They'd sometimes get halfway, turn around and come the other way," he recalls. "On the other side there were baking dogs, sometimes we really had hell getting them across."

Fimbel recalls that his uncle had two teams of mules

that he used at the feedlot to haul up cottonseed meal and hulls from the cake factory located in the vicinity of the present power plant. Floyd Peoples was one of the drivers.

"You could go by there in the morning and smell that cottonseed stuff steaming," he says. "All we fed in those days was plain cottonseed or meal and hulls."

Sometimes when it was wet, the mules could hardly pull the heavily loaded wagons back to the pens.

Fimbel recalls that the blood from the slaughterhouse was run out to the hog pens in a long trough, that sometimes the mules would go around and drink it, and they always stayed as slick as a shiny new silver dollar.

The hogs also got the guts, hauled out to them by wagon.

In his younger days, Fimbel used to do some roping, along with his brother, Chink, some others like Bill Lipscomb, Claude Mullins and Bennett Dincans. Would head out early on a Sunday morning and rope all day long at one of the arenas in the area. Jackpots weren't big in those days, not at two to four bits a throw, but they had a lot of fun.

Had to do something after working cattle all week.

Fresh as Could Be
(February 4, 1996)

There was no ground meat.

Not at the Linburg Market where Ben Klump began a long career in the butcher and livestock business as a teenage boy back around 1916.

Klump worked several years for the Linburg brothers, Gilbert, Calvin and Robert, at their slaughterhouse on the north edge of Goliad and at a market where they sold meat on the east side of the courthouse square.

"Whoever heard of hamburger meat," he says. "Only time you got hamburger was when a carnival was in town."

They did have stew meat, but mostly the market sold steaks, roasts and ribs, whatever the customer wanted, cut by the chunk.

"We didn't have a scale," he recalls. "We would cut off 50 cents or a dollar's worth, whatever you wanted. A dollar would buy a lot of roast."

They also made beef sausage every day, with a steam-powered cutter.

"Fresh meat and sausage was all we sold," he says, "and we sold lots of it."

Klump would work some 40 or more years in the butcher business and in buying, selling, trading and hauling livestock, before becoming a Goliad County deputy sheriff from 1961 to 1977. He then worked security for five more years at Schroeder Hall.

Born in 1901 in Austin County, his family moved when he was six weeks old to a farm about three miles north of Goliad and into town during a drought that started in 1915.

He can remember when a butcher came around in a wagon with fresh meat when they were still on the farm.

When he went to work for the Linburgs, as he recalls, they had the only meat market in Goliad.

"I made many a pound of sausage," he says.

The sausage was sold in links, and one of his jobs at the slaughterhouse was cleaning the intestines for use as sausage casings.

"Them guts were clean when we got through with them," he says.

The market was rather simple, with sausage hanging on side racks, a butcher block, and a table on which the meat was laid out each morning behind a screen from which customers were served.

When he first went to work, the market didn't have a cooler. They would butcher in the evening and let the meat cool overnight in a screened enclosure, then haul it by wagon to the market early in the morning.

"We opened up way before daylight," he recalls. "In them days, you would be surprised how many people wanted steak for breakfast."

If the market had meat left over, which usually wasn't much, they would take it that night to Jecker's Ice House, and did that until the Linburgs got their own cooler.

"We used a block and tackle to put four or five 300-pound blocks of ice on top of it," Klump says. "That was the worst job of the whole thing."

His work included driving cattle to the slaughterhouse, in those days there being no other way to get them there, and he remembers once bringing a herd of 50 fed steers from Goldman Hill at Victoria to Goliad.

"We saddled up at one in the morning," he says, "and got back just as the sun was going down."

They butchered all grown cattle — "the bigger the better" — cows, heifers and steers.

"The customers would quit buying if they thought it was bull meat," he recalls.

With a steak, roast or ribs, the market would give the customer a soup bone, a customary practice in markets for many years, or perhaps some liver, although he says they could hardly give the liver away and most of it was fed to the hogs.

The slaughterhouse had a hog pen, which by law had to be 100 feet away, but close enough so the blood could be run in a wooden chute. The hogs got whatever couldn't be used otherwise.

Hides were sold, and Klump recalls they were worth more at times than the Linburgs paid for the cattle.

The Linburgs' father, Herman, an old hide and tallow man, had started the market. Klump's sister, Freida, had married one of his sons, Gilbert.

A lot of changes would take place during Klump's career in the livestock and meat business, from meat markets being incorporated into grocery stores to modern refrigeration and packaging, but there is something that can be said for the old markets.

The meat was as fresh as could be.

XIII

THE DEPRESSION

Dollar Well Worn
(May 20, 1980)

There we were sitting around the table, drinking 35-cent coffee and discussing the state of the economy, when someone brought up the Great Depression.

Get to talking about economic conditions and the conversation invariably turns in that direction, those years during the late 20s and the 30s having made such an impact on those who lived through them.

I got in on the end of the Depression — makes me a Depression baby, I guess, already something of an antique — but due to my tender age at the time I was fairly well insulated from the full impact of what was going on around me.

Didn't know at the time that we were poor, that virtually everyone was poor, even some of those that we thought of as being rich at the time.

There is one thing I've noticed about those who lived through the Depression, those who were old enough to have to make a living, and that is most of them have a greater respect for the dollar than those of us who were born during that period or came along later.

Among those around the coffee table was Phil North, who pulled a silver dollar out of his pocket, something he's been carrying around with him for some 45 years now. The date is even worn off, but ever since he's had it he hasn't been broke. Says he can remember a time when all he had wouldn't add up to a dollar otherwise. Wouldn't have bought a cup of coffee at today's prices.

Lot of others can remember when they didn't have a dollar to their name either, nor know where their next one was coming from.

Phil's dollar was fresh on my mind a day or two later when Jack Zawacki of Edna got to telling me about some of his experiences during the Depression, when he was just as broke and practically freezing to death on a freight train that he'd caught in Butte, Montana, or some place like that. Had strapped himself to the catwalk with his belt so he wouldn't fall off the car he was riding, should he fall asleep or the cold get the best of him. Went all the way to the West Coast.

Met Zawacki quite by accident when I drove by the place on Elm Street where he and his wife, Cecilia, live and operate some adjoining apartments. What caught my eye was three big red, white and blue rockets sticking out of the ground, enough to slow anyone down. Saw this man drilling holes in some sheet metal behind the apartment building, had to stop and find out what he was up to.

He used to be in the restaurant business and is what's usually referred to as being semi-retired, but has to find something to keep busy or he's not happy. He had salvaged an old gin and used some of the metal to make the rockets, gave him something to do.

When he bought the old Texana Apartments, they were in a sad state of repair, so Zawacki set about fixing them up. Does all the repair work himself.

That's another thing I've noticed about those who went through the Depression. Not only do they seem to have more respect for the dollar than most of the rest of us, but they seem to be able to do more things on their own. Guess once a person has had to do it, it becomes a way of life.

Recall one of my uncles once telling me that he couldn't have made it through the Depression if it hadn't been for his milk goat. Wouldn't have had the money to buy milk for the kids.

Doubt if I could get a goat to give me any milk, know I could never have fixed up that apartment building, or built those rockets. Certainly haven't been able to hold onto a dollar long enough to wear it out.

If there is ever another Depression, sure hope there is a demand for someone to write about it.

Ruf' Old Days
(March 17, 1988)

Don't imagine 50 years or so from now that anyone will be looking back at these past few years as hard times. Not that a lot of folks haven't suffered, even some of the wealthy like John Connally and that doctor fellow in Houston who lost so much real estate, and it has certainly been tough in the oil patch, but nothing like what we generally look back on as the hard times.

More specifically, the Great Depression.

I think a person had to be there to really appreciate what happened, and I'm certainly too young to remember much about it myself, having been born toward the tail end if it, but those of retirement age today can remember and I hardly know a one of them who doesn't have some fears about it happening again, which I think is one reason they represent such a thrifty and hardworking generation.

A. Doyle Cannon sent me some of his thoughts on the subject here awhile back, and I'd like to share some of what he says, especially with the younger folks who might not have a real feeling for the way it was back then — "in the ruf' old days," as he says. He's a Depression kid, having been born in 1922, and says he can remember his dad walking the streets of Muskogee, Oklahoma, for two years looking for work which wasn't to be found.

There was no unemployment insurance, no food stamps, no real welfare, and he says people had to do their best on their own and that he remembers praying that one day his dad would come home with a job, and finally he did find work with Griffin Grocery Co. at $10 a week, minus ten cents for Social Security, leaving $9.90 to raise a family of four on.

Cannon says it was a time that left scars that will never heal — "a feeling of insecurity, regardless of what we now have — down deep, we remember, and are afraid — fearing it could happen again."

"I managed to work my way through high school, via a paper route — went into the Navy, came back, graduated from college, got a good job — but always felt insecure — still do," he says, even though he is now retired after working for many years in the grocery business, including managing supermarkets and retiring as district manager of a big grocery chain.

Retired and now living in Victoria, he says everything is comfortable, but yet, way back in his mind, he is afraid.

"Afraid of what the Depression did to me, to my parents — afraid it might hit again — though the experts say, 'no way,' but those experts did not live through the Depression like I did — they do not know it all — how bad things got," he writes. "They do not wake up at night, sweating, worrying, etc. — about another depression."

Cannon says he doesn't know how much money it would take for him to feel completely secure in this old world, but it would be a lot.

I think he sums up pretty good about how people of his generation feel, and he also talks a bit about how they got through it.

"One time in Muskogee, right in the middle of the Depression, all we had to eat came out of our little garden," he recalls. "We had vegetable soup and hot biscuits for supper most nights — no meat. And sometimes we had poke greens, pulled from out in the country, wherever we could find it. Seems too, back then, we found wild lettuce, or what we called wild lettuce."

Later on, he said, when times got a bit better, on Sundays his mother would fix a meat loaf, which was the only day they had meat. In later years, he said they moved up to a piece of round steak — also, on Sundays only — and he was grown up before he ever had a whole steak of his own like a T-bone or filet mignon. To this day, however, he says meat loaf and round steak are among his favorites.

Somehow I can't see the kids of today ever feeling the same way.

Surely not about meat loaf.

The Way It Was
(October 19, 1986)

Natural childbirth has become rather popular again in recent times, but certainly not for the same reasons of necessity that prevailed in the Depression years of the 30s and times before.

"Midwifery was a common practice during that era," Ethel Prince recalls, explaining that among black families birthing was also quite a ritual. It was one of many topics of black culture she covered recently as one of the participants in the storytelling at the VictoriaFest.

When the baby was born, she says, both mother and child were placed in a dark room, and for 30 days the mother was virtually held prisoner, although she says on the ninth day it was customary to take the mother outside and let her walk around, if it was a good day.

"During the first nine days, both mother and child were in the dark room."

After the ninth day, she says the mother was allowed to get around the home, but shampooing of the hair, cooking, and other such chores were delayed until the baby was a month old.

"The mother was considered unclean until then," she recalls.

Also, she says, babies were often breast fed for up to two years, since there was a common belief that a mother wouldn't get pregnant again while nursing.

"The colored baby was loved and nurtured by the entire family," she says, "and as the baby's hair grew it was braided, even if the baby was a boy."

She says a little boy's hair wouldn't be cut until his first birthday, since it was thought that such would impede the child's speech development.

Those were also times when home remedies were used for most of the more common illnesses in children, and various superstitions prevailed, such as the wearing of silver dimes and even little bags of sow bugs around the neck, as a protection against colic and the pains of teething, for instance.

"As the child grew," she says, "it would also learn about the rich diet of the family, often consisting of vegetables cooked in fatback, rich gravies, home cooked breads, lots of syrup, and other foods that went a long way. The colored mother learned economics out of necessity."

Now I think a lot of us who grew up during that time, as she did, can associate with much of what she recalls about those days regardless of what race or color we might be, and those older are no doubt even more familiar with some of the things she talks about, like how sugar ants used to be such a problem, and people would actually set their table legs in small containers of water to keep the little pests from getting to the sugar and syrup on the table.

She says the colored child also learned that a bed had a head and a foot, because their families were often large and the houses small, and children slept as many as four to a bed at both ends.

Although those were hard times, and no doubt even harder for the black people than for most whites, she tells of her life as a girl without showing any of the bitterness that can cloud such memories when discussing the days prior to integration, when there were separate schools, and blacks had to sit at the back of the bus, and so forth. She said it was sometimes confusing to her, like when she rode the bus from Refugio to

Victoria and had to use a back seat, but if she caught the train at Bloomington she was required to sit toward the front. As a child she says it was sometimes difficult to understand it all, but that was the way it was at the time.

The daughter of Kathleen and Tommy Heard, who many people around Victoria know as the man who had the barbecue stand for so many years at Pleasant Green and the Port Lavaca Highway, she attended colored schools at Refugio and in Victoria, graduating from Gross High School in the early 50s. She later attended Victoria College, after the college was integrated, and taught early childhood development at St. Mark's Methodist School for seven years, but now works with her husband, Lonnie, in their pest control business.

One of the things she mentioned, and something that certainly wasn't limited to the black families, and that's how people used to starch everything, even the bed sheets were often starched, and if something wasn't starched it was certainly ironed. She recalls once when her mother was working, and being the middle sibling she was left to care for her baby sister and do some of the chores, she starched the baby's diapers.

In those days, starch was first mixed with cold water, then added to the warm water, and if it wasn't done just right it would leave lumps of starch on the clothes, and one could always spot the children at school whose clothes weren't starched properly. Also, in those days, long broomstick skirts were in style and the starching would help the skirt stand out.

"We'd go to school just a rattling," she recalls.

I've just touched on some of the things she talked about, and one thing that she leaves no doubt about, even out of the hardest of times she gained a lot of pleasant memories. Believe I learned more about the black culture listening to her in just a few minutes than I had ever known before. I'm also a child of the 30s and in many ways I guess we were all segregated.

Yet, there were lots of things we all had in common.

Got me to wondering now when I got my first haircut, although I do remember from what I've been told that I put up quite a fuss.

Speech must have been developed pretty good by then.

XIV

HOME BREW

In a Crock
(May 23, 1990)

Anita Huck was saying how she used to get out of picking cotton.

"Chopping, or whatever," she said. "When my dad had home brew about ready."

Saw her at Nordheim during the May Fest at the Shooting Club.

When the red line on the tester got near where it was supposed to be, she says her dad, Anton Riebschlaeger, would make her stay at home to keep an eye on it.

She said he made the home brew in a "big ol' crock."

Later Elsa Leister brought up the subject of home brew, which gets me to thinking that there sure must have been a lot of it around Nordheim back when.

Mrs. Leister was telling how she snuck a drink once.

When she was a young girl, of course.

"I was about 13," she recalls. "I went upstairs where dad kept his home brew and got me a cup of beer out of the crock."

I asked her what her parents had to say about it later.

"They didn't say anything," she said. "They didn't know I drank it."

Her dad, Willie Buesing Sr., kept his home brew in the attic at the time, and she was recalling one time when it began to pop and drip through the roof on the dining table.

To keep it cool, she says he would also lower the bottles into a cistern at times in a tow sack.

"And," she adds. "One time we had it under the

house. He would put down a layer of hay with some tow sacks over it, pour water on it, then put the beer bottles on top of the sacks.

"Then he'd put some more tow sacks and hay on top of the beer."

She says once she was sent home from the field to set the table and heard something pop under the house and thought someone had fired a shot.

"I ran to the field to tell daddy," she recalls. "He said it was just a bottle of beer going off."

Mrs. Leister was at the cook-off in conjunction with the annual May Fest, which always includes a softball tournament, dance, and other activities. When I talked to her, she'd just paid $50 at auction for a pint of first place chili cooked by her daughter-in-law, Shirley, who with her husband Ray Leister operates Nordheim's historic Broadway Bar.

Speaking of chili, I also got to visit for awhile with Leo and Leona Buehring of Runge, whose daughter, Pat Irvine of Seguin, just happens to be the executive director of the Chili Appreciation Society International.

Bill Reader was there from Runge, and was one of the judges. He was telling me about someone out his way who claims to have stolen a bunch of cows once, bought feed for them on credit and didn't intend to pay the bill, and later took them to the auction and lost money on the deal.

Someday I've got to meet that fellow.

Reader probably has a few cotton pickin' stories he could tell, but he was too busy tasting the chili, beans, and barbecue to talk much.

I had thought about writing another cotton pickin' column myself for today, but about all I could get anybody to talk about was home brew.

It could have been the heat, because it was hot and that's the kind of weather after a hard day in the field that would make a person want to go to the well for a cool one or dig under the house.

Maybe put some in a tub for the May Fest.

I just get the feeling that when the occasion was right there wasn't any shortage of something cool to drink around Nordheim.

Unless too many bottles popped all at once.

Well Cooled
(August 30, 1989)

Melvin Christen tells how they used to cool home brew in the well.

"In a Triangle flour sack," he said. "Mother would double sew it with Number 8 thread."

That was in the late 30s, he recalls, when the family lived near Moravia and flour was $3.65 for a 98-pound bag.

He said they would hang the home brew just above the water line and it would be cool when they came out of the field and needed a drink.

A bunch of us were standing around talking at Kenneth Henneke's camp last week where Gibbe Gerdes, Henneke and Charlie Straus were having their annual birthday stew, something that's been happening now for 20 years, and there was a big crowd gathered as usual. Two fellows from the new Texas Domino Association, Frank and Jackie Kirk, even came all the way from Dallas to present Gerdes an award for his work with the Texas State Championship Domino Tournament in Hallettsville, which he helped start 35 years ago, as well as all he's done since to promote dominoes in Texas.

As usual, they had plenty of good stew at the party even though Christen says he wasn't able to catch enough turtles for the soup. He generally provides the main ingredient for the turtle soup, but the turtles just didn't seem to be around, possibly because of the drought.

Even that country back in there where Henneke's camp is located, south of Rabb Switch between Hallettsville and Sublime, is showing the effects of the dry weather this year, except there is a good crop of Spanish moss on the trees, which always reminds me of sauerkraut.

Speaking of sauerkraut, that's another topic we got to talking about somehow, think it was after Calvin Albrecht mentioned that Leonard Christen's wife, Pat, and her mother, Annie Honish, are good at putting up kraut. Mrs. Honish is also known around that area for the welder's caps she makes.

Leonard is Melvin's son.

Melvin says when he was a boy, back there about the same time they were putting the home brew in the well, that his family would put kraut down in a 3-gallon crock using a stomper from the butter churn to pack it. In between, he says, about every four inches, they would put a layer of pickles. He and his brother, Joe, dug a hole around the edge once to get to the pickles, but his mother noticed what they'd done and threatened to tell his dad.

"We didn't do it anymore," he recalls.

Christen said they had 11 in the family — "nine children and mom and dad" — and ate a lot of kraut.

He said they weighed down the kraut with the bottom of an oak barrel, with a big rock on top.

"I think that rock is still in the attic," he says. "I still have the crock, the stomper, and the butter churn."

Albrecht, who is the district clerk in Lavaca County, says his dad, Frank, a native of Austria, had a big petrified rock that he put on top of a grass sack to weigh down his kraut.

Driving back out toward Hallettsville later, past a big mossy oak, I thought how the hanging moss really does look a bit like sauerkraut and I was reminded of an old joke which you've probably heard anyway.

Would be easy to pick.

XV

MUDDY ROADS

Detour Ahead
(January 31, 1988)

It's getting harder and harder to find a muddy road.

When I was first learning to drive a car, along about 1951 or 1952 — actually, I started with a Ford tractor, but everybody doesn't have to know that — all that was needed was a rain and you'd have a muddy road. I can remember when we'd slip and slide for a mile just trying to get out of the yard at times, and if we were lucky enough to get to the road that's when the fun really started.

Don't get me wrong — some of you older folks — I wasn't even born yet when roads were really bad, although when I was real little and we lived near Airville and Zabcikville in Bell County we had some that I think would stack up with the roads down here, even in the blacklands below Victoria where it was something else to get around during wet months. I just barely remember the roads back in the 30s, before we moved out to West Texas where they had good roads because of two things — first, it didn't rain a lot. Second, they had lots of caliche which makes a good surface on country roads, although I have seen it get pretty soft, and it will get slick.

Remember the first time I ever drove around Victoria

County, after we moved here in 1963, and how I was amazed that many the country roads — not just the farm-to-market roads — were blacktopped. In all of West Texas, I had never seen anything like it, but after the first long rainy spell I began to realize why.

There were advantages to the muddy roads, of course, especially after the days when the school buses started running and if it rained enough a lot of times we didn't have to go to school, even where we had the caliche. It was also a lot of fun, if you weren't driving, and if the car happened to slip out of the ruts and into the ditch it gave everybody something to talk about for a week or more. I remember one particular time we were all in a Model-A Ford being driven by one of my uncles when a mouse ran out from under the seat and he let the car slip off into the ditch.

I think of that to this day as a major event in my life, which just goes to show how little it really took back then to cause some excitement, and if we'd turned over it would have really been something. As it was, there was enough yelling and screaming going on to make a kid think that he'd never live to see the first grade. Nobody got hurt, except for the mouse.

Slipping into the ditch and getting stuck in itself wasn't all that unusual, which I would learn as time went on, as I would also learn that it's really not as much fun driving in mud as it looks when you're not the one behind the wheel. I just never quite got the knack of it myself, especially when it came to figuring if I should follow the existing ruts, or make a new set. What I did learn is that you can get stuck either way.

Mud chains, that's something else you don't see much anymore, and I'd imagine a lot of the younger folks have probably never seen them at all, but when I was growing up if a long rainy spell came it would bring out the chains. By the time I was driving we never used them, but by then most folks out in the country had pickup trucks and mud-grip tires. Earlier, I remember Dad would sometimes put them on the car. When we got on the highway, we would sling mud the rest of the way into town.

Then there was the road detours, another thing we don't see as much today, or at least not where you have to drive for miles and miles on graded surfaces or less. Once I remember we must have spent half our time on detours while on a trip to Waco, after the war years when there was a lot of road construction going on. Now they just build a new road beside the old one, and there is hardly any inconvenience at all, except maybe out in some area where they don't have the traffic to warrant it — know we got on a pretty rough strip of highway work year before last on a trip to Terlingua.

One last thing, the low water crossings are pretty well gone — on the highways at least, and even on most country roads. I'm told that back in the old days if it came a pretty good rain you might as well forget about traveling for awhile between Victoria and Goliad, or Refugio either, as far as that goes, because of the low crossings on Coleto Creek where the soft sand would sometimes make it difficult to cross even for days afterward, except there was usually somebody near the creek who just happened to have a good team of horses or mules. Same held true for creeks all over the country, but that's just the way it was.

If somebody had told me, even in the 50s when I was at an age to still enjoy mud, that the day would come when young people would be buying big-wheel vehicles just to go looking for it, so they could have some fun driving in it, I wouldn't have believed it.

Least we got to miss a day of school now and then.

When the Creek's Up
(July 10, 1984)

L.A. Smart was telling a little about the way it was around Raisin and Cologne when he was a boy growing up there in the teens and 20s.

Met Smart at the Goliad Stampede.

He and his wife Clara were there for the big doings over the weekend and to visit with son Fant, and he also had along some of his whatnots he makes, little rocking chairs out of clothespins and that sort of thing. Smart is retired now, worked as an X-ray technician for 25 years, then eight years as a guard for the Texas Department of Corrections at the Wynne Unit. They live in Huntsville.

Smart said his folks used to live about a mile south of Cologne on Fleming Prairie, and that he caught the mixed train many times out of Cologne where Monroe Hall and his wife, Emma, used to run the depot. He recalls everyone called them Aunt Emma and Uncle Monroe. Kathy Young had the post office on the south side of the tracks west of the depot.

He said Raisin also had a depot back in those days, a cotton gin or two, couple of dance halls, two saloons, a pool hall, barbershop, blacksmith shop, and Otto Kohl's two-story general mercantile store. Been told that store is still out around there somewhere in a pasture being used as a hay barn.

Smart said there was a dance hall there at one time run by a Mrs. Friedrichs, and it was there that he learned to dance. He said it was a rather modern dance hall for those days, even had indoor toilets.

"They used to have some hellacious barbecues at the old Friedrichs dance hall, usually on the Fourth of July," he recalls. "They'd work all year putting up canned goods, and have the barbecue cooking over a big trench. They'd turn the meat with pitchforks. It was 65 cents for all you could eat."

He can remember when they used to go to the dances there in a two-horse surrey, also when they had to cross the creek when it was up, would tie up the horses and walk the railroad bridge. Wasn't nothing except a low water crossing on the Coleto back then. He said his papa and his grandpa used to haul freight between Victoria and Goliad and were used to the mud, said his dad talked about how the horses and mules would make popping sounds as their hooves went in and out of the mud when they were pulling a heavy load.

His dad was Mark Smart, and grandpa was G.B.

Smart said he can remember when old man Charlie Stedtler would hang around the creek with a team of mules to help people cross, during the Model-T days. He said some drivers would put a big piece of cardboard in

ROADS-RUTS-AND MUD! — IF YOU'VE BEEN DRIVING A CAR THIS LONG YOU'LL REMEMBER THAT A DRIVE ON ANY PUBLIC ROAD OFTEN MEANT A "LIFT" FROM A NEARBY FARMER AND HIS LIVESTOCK!
— STICKS STAHALA

front of the radiator to keep from drowning out, then bulldoze their way across. But that didn't always work, and old Charlie would be in business. Sometimes they'd hooraw him a little, insinuate that he'd been sneaking out there at night and digging the holes deeper.

After he got 'em across, we'd expect.

Follow the Ruts
(March 7, 1996)

Leon J. Berkovsky tells how one got to Providence.

When the roads were bad after a rain, as he remembers them often being when he was teaching for a year in the school community about seven miles down river from Hallettsville, all one could do was follow the ruts.

"It seemed like 30 miles," he recalls. "There was no use trying to stay out of the deep ruts caused by previous cars, possibly even wagons.

"The procedure was to drive until the car wheels fell into the ruts, then put it in low gear, take one's hands off the steering wheel and slowly progress down the road, hoping that one did not encounter a vehicle coming from the other direction."

Berkovsky drove a 1929 Model-A coupe which he had purchased for $35.

"It had narrow tires and large diameter wheels" he says, "and was a real 'mudder.'"

A resident of Vienna, Virginia, Berkovsky has many fond memories, other than for the rutty roads, of his year teaching at the Providence School and of growing up in Lavaca County around Sweet Home and in the South Mustang School community from which he recalls being the first individual to attend high school eight miles away at Yoakum.

He graduated form Yoakum High School in 1939.

"I rode a horse in the 10th grade," he says, "and a bicycle in the 11th. There was no 12th grade then."

Afterwards he attended Southwest Texas Teachers College at San Marcos and took the teaching job for the school year 1941-42 with some 13 students in nine grades, although not all grades had students.

He sends along a recent picture of the old frame building, still standing, but badly leaning, taken by a former Providence student, Dennis R. Janak of Brazoria.

Berkovsky fished and hunted bullfrogs with Janak's father, Laddie.

He boarded with a "Mrs. Larke, or Larky, and her son, Sonny," and remembers there was also an elderly man known as Captain John who took his evening meals with them.

"He always rode a beautiful spirited gray horse and wore an expensive white Stetson hat," Berkovsky recalls. "He rode in a proud manner as if he was some ancient Roman warrior."

Berkovsky applied for the teaching job and was hired by one of the school trustees, Joe Steffek, who conducted a brief interview while working in a field with his family.

After World War II and 50 missions as a navigator, and being a prisoner of war after his B-17 "Flying Fortress" was shot down after a raid on a German aircraft factory at Vienna, Austria, he attended the University of Texas where he received a degree in architectural engineering in 1949, which resulted in a career as a construction manager that took him around the country.

But, regardless of where he was at, Berkovsky has always remembered with fondness the years that he spent growing up around Sweet Home, Yoakum and Hallettsville, and that year at Providence.

"I had a great time there," he recalls.

Reminds me of the old saying, that you can take the boy out of the country, but you can't take the country out of the boy.

Works the same way with being a Texan.

XVI

AGE OF THE AUTOMOBILE

From Model-Ts On
(April 21, 1991)

Drove out Paco Road and found Herman Johnson under his chinaberry tree working on a lawn mower.

I guess you could call him a shade tree mechanic now.

Johnson spent years working on automobiles before he retired in the 1970s after 37 years with Atzenhoffer Chevrolet in Victoria, but he started out way back in 1926 working for Wacker Garage in Yoakum on mostly Model-T Fords.

He was just a boy at the time, 13 or 14 years old, when Wacker hired him.

"I was working at the flour mill helping sweep," he recalls. "There was a gin right close to it, and I went home and built me a model gin. Wacker saw what I'd done and asked my dad if I might like to work on cars."

Johnson said he got all the money he made on flats, a percentage on the oil, and a commission on any other work he did up until about when he got married in 1928 to Angelyn Mikeska. Wacker then put him on a regular salary of $10 a week.

He later worked for the International Harvester dealers in Yoakum and Port Lavaca, before coming to

Victoria to work for Atzenhoffer in 1937.

"I was up to 40 cents an hour," he recalls. "After awhile I got a raise to 55 cents and stayed at that for a good many years, until we went on commission."

He said the mechanics also had to stand by their work.

Johnson said he'd been driving cars since he was about 12 years old, since they had a neighbor at Yoakum who had a Model-T, but only drove it once a month to Harlingen to see his girlfriend.

"The rest of the time it just sat there," he says. "He started letting me drive it when I was about 12. Then he let me have it to go to dances."

In his early days with Wacker, Johnson says he worked on all kinds of cars, Fords, Chevies, a few Stars, Oldsmobiles, Rios, Buicks and Dodges, whatever happened to be on the road at the time.

He particularly remembers how much time he had to spend overhauling Model-Ts.

"It would take three days sometimes to fit the bearings on the crankshaft," he says. "We had to pour in melted lead and then shape it with a special spoon that was sharp on both sides. It was a job to fix the Model-T back in those days."

It's said Model-Ts could be tied together with baling wire, and he says that's particularly true.

"I cut many a piece of old barbed wire alongside the road to tie up motor supports on Model-Ts," Johnson recalls.

Mechanics did road service in those days and well past the time of the Model-T, like he was recalling once when he had to go work on a lady's Buick just this side of McFaddin. A spring had broken in her distributor.

"She had a hair pin," Johnson says. "I fashioned it to make enough tension on the points for her to drive into town."

He said about all a mechanic needed for road work was a pair of pliers, a screwdriver, and a couple of end wrenches.

"Road service meant road service," he says. "I did lots of jobs on the road. I went out to Foster Field once when it was freezing cold to do a rear hub bearing on a truck trailer and like to froze to death. That's one time I purt'near quit."

He once worked on a car for Tex Ritter. The cowboy movie star had his oil changed in Port Lavaca and someone forgot to replace the plug, and Johnson says Ritter's engine burned up between there and Victoria.

"I put a short block in his Buick," he recalls, "and had him ready to go that same day."

Johnson says he quit working on cars but still does some small engine repair beneath his chinaberry tree, where I found him and a cloud of mosquitoes following the recent rains.

"They don't bother me as long as I'm moving," he said.

We went in the house to talk.

Lengthy Career
(May 22, 1996)

Fred Stockbauer got into the automobile business right out of Patti Welder High School.

When he was graduated in 1930 at the age of 16, his brother, John, had a one-man garage in an old livery stable at 207 W. Constitution across from the present Victoria County tax office, which wasn't there at the time.

Stockbauer recalls there were still names on the wall of the owners of the horses that were once stabled there.

"John said he couldn't pay much, but would give me five cents an hour," Stockbauer recalls, "and lunch."

He worked six days a week from 7 a.m. to 6 p.m. for $3 a week.

"I happened to buy an old motorcycle for $5 and got it fixed up," he says. "I had to put tires on it."

It took about three gallons of gas a week, at about 18 cents a gallon, to go the five miles up the Upper Mission Valley Road to the home place, otherwise he didn't have many expenses and tried to save a dollar a week from his salary.

"By 1933," he recalls, "I was making $10 a week. Then, President Roosevelt put in the minimum wage and I went to $14 a week."

Tractors were just coming in and Victoria Hardware had the Farmall dealership and the garage did their repair work.

Stockbauer remembers how dusty it was during those days, that being during the time of the Dust Bowl when even the sun was blotted by dust as far away as New York.

John Stockbauer, who had become a partner with Anton Stanzel, sold his interest to his brother in 1936 and went into the tractor business.

During the early part of World War II, Stanzel sold his interest to Richard Zeplin.

"We began stocking Hudson parts since there was no dealership in Victoria," Stockbauer recalls. "At the end of 1945, when the factory started back to building cars, we got the Hudson dealership and built a showroom to the east side of the old livery stable."

At the time, their back door was opposite that of another automobile dealer, Atzenhoffer Chevrolet and Buick, located in the same block at the corner of Santa Rosa and Bridge streets, where the First Victoria National Bank's drive-in facilities are now located.

Stockbauer-Zeplin also had a half-lot for used cars in the block where the new county jail is today.

They moved out on Navarro Street in 1960, building where Coca-Cola is now located, and Stockbauer remembers their bankers saying they were taking a chance "going way out in the country on the poor farm road."

They had the Buick dealership, which Atzenhoffer had given up in 1954, and added Dodge because of the demand for smaller cars. They later got the Opel, a Buick import from Germany, and let Dodge go after six years. They also sold GMC pickups and trucks.

Stockbauer sold his interest in 1973 after 43 years in the automotive business in Victoria.

In the early days, he remembers completely rebuilding Model-A Ford engines with all new parts, except for the block, crankshaft and camshaft, for $49.50.

Flat rate labor was 75 cents an hour.

"We thought it was really going up when it went to a dollar," he recalls. "You could get your brakes adjusted for 35 cents."

That, or your tappets.

XVII

OLD SALTY

A Train to the Beach
(April 15, 1988)

This time of year as the weather starts to warm, some of us start thinking about the beach.

That's nothing new, and about all it takes to get there is to ice down a cooler and hop in the car, most anyone in the area can be sunning on the beach or fishing in the surf within minutes, an hour at the most. Wasn't always quite that easy, but it didn't keep people from going, although perhaps not as often, and sometimes the anticipation could be about as much fun as the trip itself.

We're thinking about when a lot of folks went to the beach by train.

That was before my time, but Ned Hellums of Yoakum remembers it well, and at the time he was just a boy living in Placedo where he watched the trains coming and going and got acquainted on a first name basis with some of the crews, especially the ones on Old Salty. All the old-timers in this area remember Old Salty, the train that made regular runs from Cuero to Port Lavaca in the 20s. Hellums says it was a mixed train, composed of a passenger coach, a mail car, and on an average from one to five boxcars loaded with freight.

He recalls Henry Sanders was the engineer, a man affably known as "Uncle Henry." Hellums describes him as a clean-cut pudgy type with a well-trimmed mustache, white cap and overalls of blue.

"When stopping in Placedo to unload freight or passengers," he recalls, "Uncle Henry would sometimes get off the locomotive and pat us kids on the head. That was a compliment for all of us."

He said Old Salty traveled on a lightweight track — about 50 or 60-pound rail — and never too fast, in fact a Model-T on the adjacent gravel road (the Port Lavaca Highway) could outrun the train if the driver was so inclined.

The big traffic to the beach, however, was on the excursion trains that often ran on weekends during the summer months and especially for the July 4th holiday, when there was always a big celebration at Port Lavaca, which had a dance pavilion on the beach in those days. The excursion trains usually had from eight to ten passenger cars, Hellums recalls, and were often so filled with passengers that it was difficult to find a seat. Also, he says, the small "tea pot" locomotives would have difficulty starting the train rolling again when they stopped at the small stations along the way.

These trains would often originate in the bigger towns, as far away as San Antonio and Houston, and sometimes there would be two excursions through Placedo on the same day, especially during the holiday weekend.

Hellums particularly remembers taking the excursion train to Port Lavaca with some relatives for the July 4th festivities when he was about five years old.

"That was an adventurous, exciting and long trip," he recalls. "Trains of this sort were able to go at least 30 to 35 miles per hour — better than a horse and buggy."

That was either in 1913 or 1914, and he says it was a beautiful weekend for going to the beach. There was a blue sky with a sprinkling of fleecy clouds, a sailboat here and there on the water.

"Men in their Long John bathing suits were wading and swimming," he recalls, "and the ladies wore bathing suits which resembled skirts, with stockings or hose."

People would swim and fish during the day, then dance at the pavilion during the evening, before catching the train for home unless they were staying over, perhaps at one of the beachfront hotels. He recalls they were back in Placedo at 1:30 a.m., and that it was a day he has never forgotten.

The kind of day that didn't come every day.

Singing in the Cars
(October 31, 1986)

Some of the old-timers around town will remember Old Salty.

That was the excursion train that ran on weekends to Port Lavaca where they had the big pavilion out over the bay, and folks would go for a day of fishing, swimming and dancing, but not necessarily in that order. Suppose over the years there were different trains, but they all became singularly known as Old Salty.

Now we're talking back before people could jump in the car and be there in a short time, in the wagon and Model-T days when a trip like that was still considered of some distance and a whole lot more trouble than taking the train. Much less the train was a lot of fun, and from an account I read recently in a volume of stories put together by the *DeWitt County View* for the Sesquicentennial year I'd say folks weren't near as stodgy back then as we're sometimes led to believe.

Willie Brieger of Orange Grove was 96 years of age in 1969 when he was interviewed about his experiences as a brakeman on Old Salty, and he died in 1976 at the age of 103. He said on the way to Port Lavaca the people were always orderly, sober and dignified, but in high spirits, anticipating a day at the seashore. The ladies would be dressed in their finest, lovely with the flush of excitement, and the men were always on good behavior in their funny suits and the Panama hats or fancy derbies of the day.

Brieger said there was usually singing in the cars, and at times there would even be whole bands or orchestras boarding the train at Cuero or Victoria.

It was the return trip that Brieger said he dreaded.

"You wouldn't believe the stunts some of those bums could pull on the train crew going home from Port Lavaca," he said. "Somebody would always disengage the cars and Old Salty would have to back up several miles and pick up the cars after stopping."

There was a brake at the rear of each car, which looked like a steering wheel, and that was often too much of a temptation for some fun loving passenger to overlook.

"Some fool would turn them and Old Salty would have to huff and puff for power to drag the braked cars before I could get a chance to unwind the brake," he recalled.

He said fights were frequent, and that the singing always continued on the way back, but it was more like a sick calf bawling by then because of the preponderance of drunks who also did their part to mess up the train when they weren't singing or fighting.

On the return trips, he said the best passengers were those who were sound asleep.

"Train crews had great difficulty because we surely expected someone to be killed by falling between the cars or off the train," he said. "It wasn't much fun going home."

Brieger said he could take care of himself with most anybody, however, but that he never did learn how to handle a drunk woman.

Every job has its problems.

Lost Cuff Link
(September 12, 1979)

Henry Hammack took one of those excursion trains to Port Lavaca back around 1915 or 1916 and lost a cuff link.

Hammack said he made the trip with either Ernest

Weaver or Herman Wilhelm, whose family operated a gin at Guadalupe where Hammack worked as a young man.

A pier led to the pavilion, Hammack recalls. He rented a bathing suit, and while changing clothes, dropped one of his cuff links through the slatted floor and it was lost in the bay.

He doesn't remember how much the excursion ticket cost him, but said "it couldn't have been much because I wasn't making much in those days."

Hammack's family had moved to Guadalupe in 1913, when he was about 17 years old. His father, R.C. Hammack, sold out and moved his family from Hutto, near Taylor in Williamson County, to farm about a mile below Guadalupe.

"He brought along a cow and a pair of mules and a bunch of feed," Hammack recalls. "Everything was loaded in one box car."

Hammack said he often came to Victoria on foot.

"It was no walk at all," he recalls. "I would stay till after night and then walk home."

Hammack, who served as a peace officer with both the city and county for some 21 years after World War II, has a lot of memories of Victoria in those early years after his family settled in the county.

There was a grocery store and post office at Guadalupe, run by J.B. Marcak, and there were gins in practically all of the nearby communities, regardless of size, to handle the many acres of cotton that were being produced at the time.

The old city square in Victoria, where the city hall now stands, had hitching racks all around and a convenient water trough "where you could give your horses a good drink before leaving town."

Main Street went almost all the way to the river, where one could cross on a wooden plank bridge on Bridge Street, near the big hardware store Frank Wagner operated.

Down Juan Linn Street, or Dutch Lane as it was

called, there were grocery stores, a gin, and plenty of saloons. It was considered the town's red light district.

The fire wagon was pulled by horses, and Hammack said it was an exciting sight to see it round corners on two wheels racing toward a fire.

"They sure had pretty horses," he recalls.

When the first two blocks of Main Street were paved from Forrest to Santa Rosa streets, the area was roped off for a big street dance.

The town was really beginning to change.

XVIII

SYRUP MAKING

Running Thick
(September 27, 1989)

Kind of weather we've been having lately makes the syrup run thick.

I like it that way.

To me it's best when it kind of stacks up on the plate, or when it's cold enough that you have to use a table knife to work it out of the neck of the bottle.

I grew up on syrup at least once a day and sometimes more.

When I was little my folks would always talk about homemade molasses and how good it was when people still made their own syrup, but by then most folks were buying it in the store and all I remember ever having at home was Karo, which does pour thick on a cold morning and is somewhat sweeter than many of the homemade sorghum syrups that I have since tasted. The old style syrups have an entirely different flavor, and while somewhat alike they're each different, depending I suppose on the cane and the cookers.

One of the younger cookers in this area, Kenneth Anderle, was telling me at Sweet Home how he got started, carrying on a tradition of his grandpa, Rudolph Janak, who was known around Charlottenburg for his syrup making.

Anderle says Frank Kuchar showed him how to cook syrup, and most of the secrets of making good syrup are in the cooking.

Several years ago the old Janak press was brought out of retirement, and Anderle says three of his uncles, Anton, Celestine, and Charlie are involved in the syrup making, as well as a neighbor and cousin, August Fikac.

"Uncle Anton planted three acres of African white this year," Anderle says, "and made 10 1/2 gallons."

He had to plant twice, because the ants got the cane the first planting, and the second planting only got a half-inch of rain during the entire growing season.

"The stalks were short," Anderle notes.

He says they also cooked some syrup for others who had cane.

They've got one of about five cane presses still in use in Lavaca County.

Rudolph Janak started making molasses about 45 years ago.

"We were married in 1944," says Mrs. Robert Anderle, the former Frances Janak and Kenneth's mother. "Dad was cooking molasses before that."

She said he bought the press from someone at Wied.

"He always planted orange cane," she says, "and Mama did the cooking. When we were making syrup, we'd all get up at 4 a.m. and work all day, sometimes until midnight.

"It would depend on when we got the last pan done."

She particularly remembers one day when her mother worked all day cooking syrup.

"After midnight, my youngest brother, Victor, was born," she recalls.

Like a lot of other things that used to happen on the farm, syrup making was a family affair and something of a social occasion each year when it came time to cut the cane and cook the molasses.

From what I gather, with the Janaks it is still something like that, with the children and grandchildren of Rudolph Janak carrying on his syrup making at Charlottenburg, and there's yet a younger generation now who will have an opportunity to learn something about it.

All I ever knew about syrup was it came out of a bottle, and that on a cold morning sometimes it didn't come easy.

When you'd have to pry it out with a knife.

Still Cooking
(August 28, 1996)

There was a time when a person didn't have to go far to find some sorghum syrup.

Thousands of acres of sweet sorghum were planted in Texas each year for making syrup, along with sugar cane for both syrup and sugar, the latter being mostly in the eastern and southeastern counties while the sorghum was grown throughout the state.

Now, with the exception of some sugar cane production for milling in the Rio Grande Valley, these crops have pretty well disappeared with the exception of small acreages of sorghum that are individually grown for syrup.

A few farmers continue to grow sorghum for syrup in Lavaca County, and Gilbert Mozisek, off the Vysehrad School Road about six miles northwest of Hallettsville, started making syrup in 1994 when his wife, the former Evelyn Pavlicek, inherited a sorghum press built in 1904 and he had a new stainless steel vat built for cooking the syrup.

He got some help from Robert Sciba in setting it up and both have grown some sorghum, although the drought got Sciba's acre of sorghum this year. With the recent rains, he may get a late cutting, however. Mozisek harvested off his acre of African white and sugar drip sorghums, but the production was way off normal.

They also cook for others and this year had only three customers, all of them combined having only about 100 gallons of syrup compared to 500 last year.

"We just do it to keep the family tradition going," Mozisek says.

Their mothers are sisters, the former Emily and Frances Holik of Moravia, or Mrs. Joe Mozisek and Mrs. Herman Sciba, respectively.

It is also a matter of family tradition with the Janak family in the Charlottenburg area about eight miles northwest of Hallettsville, where for many years Rudolph Janak cooked syrup for family and neighbors.

One of the family who has helped carry on the tradition, David Wagner of Wied, says his grandfather would cook for three months, sometimes day and night, and have wagons of cane stacked waiting to be pressed and cooked.

"He cooked syrup for five cents a gallon," Wagner says.

He quit about the mid-1960s and the old equipment just stood there for 20 years, until Wagner's uncles, Anton, Charlie and Celestine Janak, decided to start cooking again.

Charlie's son, Michael, built a new cypress wood and stainless steel vat to replace the old galvanized vat, and since then cooking syrup has once again been a family affair, although Wagner had the only sorghum this year and it didn't do well because of the drought.

He cooked one batch of 17 gallons where last year he made 65 gallons off the same acre and a half.

Wagner baled some of his sorghum that he didn't strip and has been feeding it to his cattle, which like the sweet taste, and with the recent rains the sorghum is coming out again and he may get some more hay off his little sorghum patch.

He has been involved with sorghum and syrup making for about 10 years and plants the African white variety.

While it ceased years ago to be an agricultural

commodity of significance in Texas, the tradition of sorghum syrup making continues in Lavaca County.

Deep rooted in family tradition.

Good Memories
(August 29, 1996)

Yesterday's column reminded Dorothy Smith how good sorghum syrup could taste.

Like when it was mixed with bacon drippings and mopped up from the breakfast plate with homemade bread, back when just about everybody in the country had sorghum syrup, home-cured bacon and homemade bread, all of which she was reminded of while reading about the few who still grow sweet sorghums for making syrup in Lavaca County where she did a lot of her growing up during the years of the Great Depression.

Now of Victoria, she was a Shimek, sister of the late polka and waltz musician Wence Shimek and one of nine children of Louis and Frances Shimek.

She grew up around St. John's and Moravia in Fayette and Lavaca counties, where her dad raised sorghum cane which he would take to be pressed and cooked west of St. John's where the Kubos family had a press and cooking vat.

"Us kids would have to go out in the field and strip the cane," she recalls.

Her dad would cut the stalks and they would be standing in line with arm loads to put in the wagon.

She says they would all be wondering who would get to ride with him next to the syrup mill.

"I remember the sound of the syrup bubbling in the cooking vat," she says, "and the smell of it cooking."

After the juice was squeezed out of the stalks, in those days by a cane press powered by a horse or mule walking in circles around it, it would be cooked into syrup and put in jars.

"We always had half-gallon jars," she recalls.

They would usually make enough syrup to last until the next season.

"We had hogs, chickens, and belonged to a meat club," she recalls, the meat clubs being where farmers would butcher calves on a schedule so members could have fresh beef, and she says they had a screened-in area on the coolest part of the front porch in which the meat could be kept overnight or for a short time during the winter.

That was all before families had refrigerators in their homes.

During the Depression years, farm families pretty well lived on what they raised and sorghum syrup was just part of it.

According to my birth-year copy of the Texas Almanac of 1936, the state had 35,000 acres of sweet sorghum for syrup the previous year, along with 8,000 acres of sugar cane, with the two crops producing 1,820,000 and 1,240,000 gallons of syrup, respectively, valued at 50 to 60 cents a gallon.

While not one of the major agricultural commodities, sorghum and sugar cane syrups were important as home-manufactured products in Texas during that time for home consumption and local markets.

For sugar, by the mid-1930s, the two mills in Texas were importing cane from Cuba, although sugar cane was used for domestic manufacture during earlier times and is now being grown in the Rio Grande Valley for a modern sugar mill at Santa Rosa.

Sweet sorghums suitable for making syrup are grown today in small patches by those such as mentioned in the Aug. 28 column who do it mostly for old-times sake and to carry on family traditions of syrup making.

To those who can remember when syrup making was more common, it does bring back some good memories of smells and tastes.

Not to mention just plain good licking.

XIX

WAR TO END ALL WARS

Flew Over France
(November 20, 1988)

Didn't get to talk to Walter Wotipka a whole lot at the recent All Veterans Day program at Praha.

He'd sat through the program, the day was getting hot, and he'd already had a pretty good morning for a 93-year-old. He and Julius Pospisil, 91, were the only two World War I veterans present. The war was 70 years ago and Pospisil got in right at the end, but Wotipka served in France as a pilot and instructor, which interests me because it was really during World War I that it was proven airplanes could be effective in combat.

Mostly, up until then, they'd been used for reconnaissance by the Army, in a skirmish with Pancho Villa on the Texas border in 1916, with dubious results, and the United States was well behind its European allies in the development of combat aircraft when our nation entered the war to end all wars. Wotipka was a part of the tremendous buildup of the air forces that followed, although the war was too short for the United States to ever reach its goals, and many of the aircraft the U.S. used throughout the war were either produced or designed by European allies.

It was the beginning, however, of the great air power

we have today, and it was men like Wotipka who got it started, in a time when it could be almost as dangerous to fly as it was to be in war itself. He was primarily an instructor — and continued to fly even up until recent years — but was in France when the Armistice was signed on Nov. 11, 1918. Many U.S. pilots were being trained overseas, primarily because we were using allied aircraft.

Otto Steinhauser, service officer for American Legion Post 94 in Flatonia, who has worked many years with the All Veterans Day at Praha, did an interview sometime back with Wotipka and has sent me a copy of his story on how the young man from Flatonia ended up flying the skies over France.

Wotipka was born July 11, 1895, in Flatonia where he was also graduated from high school. He was enrolled at Texas A&M University as a junior when the United States became involved in World War I.

"One day some names were posted on the bulletin board with orders stating that these people would proceed to Leon Springs for training," Steinhauser writes. "While there he heard of a need for aviators so he requested a transfer. He was sent to the University of Texas where he studied navigation and meteorology.

"After six weeks of ground school he was sent to North Island near San Diego, California, where he started flight training in 'Flying Jennys.' They were based on an island so that a speedboat could pick up those flyers unfortunate enough to fall into the water."

Wotipka spent six months there, according to what he told Steinhauser, and was then sent to Louisiana and on to Hoboken, N.J., for two weeks before he boarded a boat for overseas.

"Three to four hundred died of the flu on the way over," Steinhauser says, "and after a very rough and hard voyage they arrived in Liverpool. The harbor was so shallow the boat was placed in a lock in order to unload. After three days in Liverpool they started across the channel with a boatload of horses. The water was so rough that many lockers and other equipment was washed overboard.

"Halfway over they had a breakdown and the boat stopped. After many anxious hours, they got it going again. Of course, German submarines were always in the channel.

"Wotipka reported to an airfield at Issoudum, near Orleans, about 120 miles south of Paris. There he was assigned as a flight instructor and started teaching other pilots."

They were flying Italian Spads with V-8 motors and French Nieuports with rotary engines, and the U.S. pilots were part of the Signal Corps. Wotipka told Steinhauser that a lot of the old-time Army men considered aircraft of dubious value, and much time on both sides of the war was spent shooting down each other's observation balloons. The planes had little effect on ground action. There were no control towers or radar, so flag men were used on the ground to control takeoffs and landings.

"Vickers machine guns were timed to shoot through the revolving propellers," Wotipka recalls, "and the pilots would steal cook stove lids from the kitchen and place them under their seats, hoping to deflect some of the ground fire which always came their way."

Among the people who Wotipka instructed was Maj. Carl "Tooey" Spaatz, who in World War II would rise to the rank of general and serve as commander-in-chief of the U.S. Strategic Air Force in Europe. Another famous person flying from his base was Quentin Roosevelt, who died jumping out of a burning plane, and there was also a French ace by the name of Gundemeyer.

Wotipka reached the rank of captain and served until May of 1919.

"He never returned to A&M," Steinhauser says, "but became a Ford dealer in Waelder. He was still flying his own little red plane up to about 12 years ago."

One of the daring young men of the wild blue yonder.

Mules in Masks
(November 16, 1994)

Mules had to have gas masks as well as the men.

During the great Meuse-Argonne Offensive of World War I, and Glenn Christian tells how his grandfather, the late August W. Groth, remembered having to put the masks on the mules first.

Otherwise, the masked men would scare the mules.

A scared mule is hard to control and it was better to get the masks on them before the men put on their own, which was a bit of war lore that I hadn't heard before.

We happened to meet up on Main Street last week during the Veterans Day parade and Christian was telling about Groth, who died in 1959 on the Nov. 11 anniversary of the World War I armistice.

Veterans Day was originally celebrated as Armistice Day, but now honors veterans of all wars.

Of Inez, Groth was Victoria County Precinct 4 commissioner for 17 years, and was also a farmer, mechanic and construction man. In World War I, he served in the American Expeditionary Force in France as a machine gunner in the 36th Infantry Division.

Christian had read my Veterans Day column on Arthur A. Hingst and some of what he had told a daughter, Elaine Rowland of Louise, about the morning of the armistice in the American trenches, and it reminded him of his grandfather's telling about the mules.

Virgil Branch Sr. is another who fought in the Argonne Forest, including a battle led by Gen. John Pershing. At 101 years of age, he was a participant in the Veterans Day parade.

He was also at Saint Mihiel, one of the main battles in northeastern France toward the end of the war.

Just last December, Branch received the World War I Commemorative Medal marking the 75th anniversary of that war. It was presented by Post 4146 of the Veterans of Foreign Wars of which he is a longtime member.

Now a resident of Twin Pines Nursing Home in Victoria, he has been interviewed many times over the years about his war experiences, such as when an enemy shell soared in and obliterated a horse-drawn wagon that he was standing near.

He also kept his World War I helmet, which carries the mark of a bullet that grazed it during one of the battles.

Branch has always said that "war is something you want to forget," yet it's not something anyone can forget and Branch has long participated in Veterans Day events.

Trained as a cavalryman, he ended up with the infantry in the 90th Headquarters Division and never got close to riding a horse in France, but did ride in rail cars that had been used to transport horses and mules.

Branch was in the worst of it when his division was sent to the front lines to relieve the Fifth Division when there were "not enough men left to bury the dead."

I am always amazed by the experiences of such men and Hingst, Groth and Branch, who in those rather simple times were called upon to fight for America in such far-off places as the Argonne Forest of France.

Like all wars, it was a war like no other.

Big Noise
(November 11, 1994)

The men could hear a big noise — a roar — off near the horizon.

At the 11th hour, on the 11th day of the 11th month of 1918, as Elaine Rowland of Louise recalls her father, the late Arthur A. Hingst, describing the Armistice morning in the trenches where he was a participant in the Meuse-Argonne Offensive.

"They wondered what it was," she said in a letter of some months ago that I put back to share with readers on this Veterans Day, once known as Armistice Day to celebrate the ending of World War I, but now a day in honor of all veterans of the armed forces.

Was it a new offensive, the men asked? Were they having a battle down along the trenches? Mrs. Rowland says her father recalled that the "roar" was moving, like a wave, along the trenches. As it got closer, the men realized it was the sound of shouting.

"The war is over, the war is over," with the words being repeated again and again. "They signed the armistice papers. We're going home."

Hingst said soldiers were throwing their helmets into the air and screaming with happiness.

"My dad's friends joined the cry," Mrs. Rowland says, "and the 'wave' continued on down the trenches."

Having been dissatisfied with simply serving as replacements for British and French troops, the Americans had been assigned a front of 85 miles from the Swiss border to the French lines and Gen. John Joseph "Black Jack" Pershing put together his All-American army for the Meuse-Argonne Offensive, a decisive part of the final Allied assault against the Germans.

The battle lasted 47 days and involved some 1.2 million Americans, with especially heavy fighting in the Argonne Forest, where the killed and wounded totaled some 120,000 men.

It was there in the Argonne where Sgt. Alvin York became such a hero when he single-handedly killed 20 Germans and captured 132 more.

I had already laid out Mrs. Rowland's letter when I happened to turn the television dial to an old movie on Sergeant York, with Gary Cooper playing York, and at about two in the morning I went to bed with eyes moist.

It is easy for me to get sentimental about such things, and the story of Sergeant York and all the other men who fought to victory in those final days of World War I is a story of great courage and American heroism.

Mrs. Rowland says her father had lied about his age to join up, a common and rather easy way to get involved in the war.

That morning in France as he and his fellow soldiers looked over the top of the trenches, they could see fires all over the battlefield.

"That was the first time in a long time there had been any heat for food or the body," she says. "He ended the story about a sniper that had been in a tree near the trenches. After Armistice was signed, he left the tree, but left behind a big mound of spent shells. I don't recall if daddy knew how many the sniper had hit during his stay in the tree."

Mrs. Rowland says her dad often told his war stories, but when young she didn't always hear them.

"I guess I thought he would always be around for me to ask if I wanted to know anything."

Once again, my eyes are moist.

Prunes and Spinach
(June 24, 1987)

The war was about over in 1918 when Claude Pfau joined up, but he got to stay a little longer.

"Everybody was getting out," he recalls, "after the Armistice on Nov. 11, and I wrote my folks I'd be home for Thanksgiving."

Then he volunteered to help in the office.

"They advanced me from private to sergeant, made me company clerk and wouldn't let me out," he recalls. "Then after my discharge I still ended up working for three weeks."

Pfau was among a group of five residents of Linwood Place who the activities director, Shelley Carnes, got together for an interview on Father's Day, and was one of two World War I veterans, the other being Earl Dietz, who saw service in Russia.

"There was more guard duty than anything else," Dietz recalls, "but some skirmishes now and then."

Dietz was born in 1896 in Kentucky, and says he was

in the building trades in Ohio, and Pfau was born in Fannin in 1896, but his family moved to Victoria in 1909.

"Dad had a general mercantile store in Sarita for a time," he says, "and later worked for Reuss Mercantile at the corner of Constitution and Liberty."

He became a meat cutter, as did another one of the group being interviewed, Frank Wheeler, from Goliad County, who also farmed for many years near Schroeder. The others were C.L. Hawkins, a retired highway patrolman from West Virginia, and Vic Segelquist, who grew up in Wharton County close to Eagle Lake, but farmed and ranched in several places and was an outstanding soil conservationist in Mills, Brown and Anderson counties. He is more recently from Palacios.

Pfau was the only one in the group with a Victoria background, and having lived here since 1909 he's seen Victoria grow from a little country town into what it is today. Right after World War I, he went into the meat market and grocery business on North Street, in the same building with the Weppler Grocery, which was just recently torn down.

Pfau's Grocery & Market had the slogan, "Everything Good To Eat."

He got his early training as a meat cutter at Simon's Market, which was on Main Street a couple of blocks from where the post office is now. Pfau says he stayed in the meat and grocery business until 1940, after that worked about eight years as a traveling auditor for Red Arrow, then spent 25 years in sales and claims for Alamo Express.

Going back to the war, Pfau said there were 65 of them that left Victoria on Sept. 18, 1918, and marched down to the depot where they got on a special coach that took them to Camp Travis, didn't get there until about eight o'clock and then they had to sit and wait about three hours for chow.

"They gave us each a tin pan," he recalls, "and all they had left was prunes and spinach."

Then he said they marched them over to a barracks where the cots had no mattresses and they had to sleep on the springs that first night, but the next day they were issued cotton mattress sacks and were marched to a big pile of rice straw.

"We were told if we liked our mattress thick to put a lot of straw in it," he recalls.

He was in the Army, and stayed there until April of 1919, since they wouldn't let him out after the war was over and he had volunteered for clerk duty.

Wouldn't even let him out after he got out.

Getting the News
(November 16, 1993)

Albert Rosenquest well remembers the day World War I ended.

Seventy-five years ago last Thursday to the day, and he and the other Rosenquest children were scrapping cotton in an effort to get the crop all picked before the worst of winter set in.

They were working in a field near Clark School, close to where the Victoria Regional Medical Center is today, and he remembers a train came by on the nearby tracks with its whistle blowing wildly.

"We didn't know what to think," he recalls.

It wasn't until several days later when his dad, Frank Rosenquest, received a copy of a semi-weekly Swedish newspaper from Austin that they realized "the war to end all wars" had come to an end.

Radio was just coming into being in Texas at the time, and many people had no telephones, especially those outside of town, so it took some days for the word to spread and the train's engineer had probably picked it up from a station telegraph operator somewhere along the line.

There was a lot of rejoicing as the news was received in the towns and cities where communication was more rapid.

Rosenquest says he remembers how wild it got along Main Street and around De Leon Plaza at the end of World War II.

"People went crazy," he recalls.

He said the traffic was bumper to bumper and people were passing liquor bottles from one to another and it appeared the whole town had turned out to celebrate.

The big celebration at the end of World War I came some months after the armistice, not only because word didn't spread as rapidly, but because the town was still recovering from the horrendous flu epidemic that first struck during the winter of 1917-18.

The disease had started up again in October of 1918 in Victoria and the city was pretty much under quarantine with a ban on public meetings.

Many of those who did get the news on armistice day defied the ban and gathered at the square where a celebration continued well into the night.

The flu ban was lifted five days later so the town had even more to rejoice about.

The big gathering, however, to welcome the returning veterans was held on June 18, 1919.

After Congress had declared war on Germany in April of 1917, many young men from Victoria and the surrounding area had joined Co. A, 5th Texas Infantry Regiment, which became Co. I, 143rd Infantry Regiment when the 36th Division was later organized.

They participated in the Meuse-Argonne Offensive that was a major factor in Germany's acceptance of the armistice.

For the June celebration, a huge "Arch of Triumph," patterned after the Arc de Triomphe in Paris, was constructed across Main Street.

Kemper Williams Sr. recalls being at the parade and has a photograph of his grandfather, George Overton Stoner, a Confederate War veteran, riding his gray horse beneath the arch.

He says the arch crossed the street from the Welder Building (First Victoria National Bank) to "Uncle Bundy" Jecker's saloon, which was adjacent to the corner drugstore that is now Bianchi Pharmacy.

That parade is still considered one of the great events in Victoria's history.

A grand day indeed.

Big Day in Victoria
(March 22, 1991)

Folks back home felt tremendously indebted.

They did all sorts of things to welcome the soldiers home after World War I, not unlike some of what we see being planned in Victoria for later on this year as more of our troops return from the Middle East, and one of the big events in 1919 was the Firemen's Parade on June 18, still considered to this day as one of the great events in Victoria's history.

It was no ordinary parade, and never before had there been such a public display of patriotism in the old town. It just seemed folks could hardly do enough to see that the returning servicemen, along with those who didn't, should be duly recognized and honored.

Not only were those from Victoria County honored, but from the surrounding area as well, and a huge "Arch of Triumph," patterned after the famous Arc De Triomphe in Paris, was constructed of wood and canvas near the intersection of Main and Constitution.

A number of Victoria's comeliest young ladies, draped as symbols of victory, posed on the facade of the arch, as through it passed the colors first, then the soldiers, and the rest of the parade. It was a great day in Victoria during a time that one writer described as being "when bands, marching soldiers, and a fluttering flag were enough to bring lumps to many throats and tears to many an eye."

Doesn't sound all that much different from 1991 to me.

It was a rather short war, in 1917 and 1918, at least compared to World War II in the 1940s, but it was still a costly one for the United States and just from Victoria County alone 39 lives were lost. Some died in battle and others from illness and other causes, especially the terrible flu epidemic that took so many lives both at home and overseas during that period. Many more soldiers died from the flu than bullets during World War I.

Many of us think of soldiers as GIs, a term from World War II in reference to "government issue," but in World War I the American soldiers were commonly called "Sammies," a term that had nothing to do with Uncle Sam, as some may think. Instead, it's said when the first troops arrived, the French yelled "viven les ashmee" — "long live our friends." It sounded to the Americans like they were saying "less Sammies."

The "Sammies" from Victoria were mostly part of the 36th and 90th Infantry divisions, although some served in other divisions and branches of the service as well.

There were many volunteers for the newly created Co. A, 5th Texas Infantry, of the Texas National Guard, which was broken up soon afterwards and became part of the new 36th Division.

Victoria County ranchman Al McFaddin did his part in recruiting by offering a $5 gold piece to any man who volunteered.

Many others were drafted, and the first from Victoria sent to France was a contingent of black soldiers who had trained at Camp Travis near San Antonio.

It was the first war where so many soldiers had to go overseas, and the citizens of Victoria and the rest of the country were prepared to royally welcome them home.

Suppose our soldiers in the recent Persian Gulf War didn't encounter anything like the Arc de Triomphe, but I guess we could spread some sand on the street.

Tie a camel at Main and Constitution.

XX

OLD-TIME BASEBALL

Boyhood Dreams
(March 3, 1983)

When I was a boy most all of us had dreams of becoming baseball players, to be like Dizzy Dean, or Joe DiMaggio, and it wasn't for the money either.

It was just about the most exciting thing a boy could aspire to be, outside of perhaps becoming president of the United States, but even then to most of us that didn't appear to be such a great job.

Seems to me that baseball has lost a lot of that excitement, not so much because of the game itself, but because of the times. We didn't have astronauts, nor space shuttles, not even much television during the time I'm speaking of, no television at all during the earlier period. Didn't have domed stadiums, outlandish contracts, nor Astro turf either.

And, when the World Series came into your living room, what excitement it was trying to imagine what all was going on from what you got from the gravel-voiced announcer on the squeaky radio, seemed the static would always pick up about the time there was a home run or some other exciting play, sometimes you would miss more of the game than you could catch.

Most of the kids in my crowd would have given up

their pitching arms just to see a professional game, then sometimes after the war we did get a minor league team in my hometown. What excitement that brought to the town, it had to be the same in Victoria with the Rosebuds, back there in the 50s. Those were still days when people would actually leave the comforts of their living rooms to go sit in an open stadium and yell and stomp and have a good time, now you couldn't get them out for a game like that if the players stood on their heads while at bat.

In the days before television, instant playbacks and prima donna contracts, a good semipro team could even attract a sizeable crowd, and there were some good ones around. There was hardly a town in Texas where on Sunday afternoon you couldn't find at least one game going on, especially in the 20s and 30s, from what I'm told. Semipro ball goes way back further than that, one of the great Victoria teams was the Safe Hits of 1905. Pitcher C.H. Wilson won 27 straight.

"Baseball back in those days was a big deal," says Raymond Weaver of Victoria, who played outfield in the 30s on the semipro Rosebuds in the Guadalupe Valley League. "Back then every town had a baseball team."

He said the teams generally did well to buy their bats and balls, but that if you could get a little rivalry going there was no problem in attracting a crowd to watch you play.

Some other Rosebud players along about then were Darrell May, Arthur Salziger, Freddy Moss, Chester and Hester Evans, N.R. Rode and the Loyd boys, Shorty, Lynn and Robert Earl, just to name a few.

They weren't the first Rosebuds either, evidently that name goes back to about 1910, when there was a minor league team organized. It was also suggested at the time that the team be called the Snaggers after all the troubles getting boats up and down the Guadalupe River, that was when Victoria still had dreams of becoming an inland port city. The name Rosebuds won out and has been carried on in Victoria baseball tradition ever since, no telling how many players both pro and semipro have played under that name, some of them going on to considerable fame.

In the early semipro days there were separate leagues for Anglo, Mexican and Negro players. There is a story that the Rosebuds at one time had a particularly dark complexioned player on the team, in one town the fans took it wrong. It's said they gave him prejudicial reason to make a home run, right out of the ballpark. The way I heard it that must have been some run.

Never even bothered to touch base.

Something Special
(August 1, 1996)

James M. Loyd, well-known locally as the old-time baseball player Shorty Loyd, remembers how Riverside Stadium came to be.

He had already been around baseball for years when after World War II, in 1946, he was encouraged by *Advocate* editor Chester Evans, local businessman W.R. McCright and City Engineer F.B. Lowry to start promoting a baseball park for Victoria.

In 1946, he says the Victoria Baseball Association was organized with Charlie Jacobson, a local oilman, as the principal benefactor, and with Loyd as baseball manager.

It was then that the postwar Victoria Rosebuds came into being, a name that had been synonymous with local baseball since the early 1900s and would continue later in the 1950s with the professional Victoria Rosebuds of the Class AA Texas League.

"Victoria businessmen were just waiting for somebody to do something to kinda put Victoria on the map," Loyd recalls. "Mayor Ben T. Jordan said, 'Shorty, we're all in agreement Victoria needs this baseball park.'"

But, he went on to point out that the city had no funds to build it, but offered land, a custodian to keep it up, and the necessary access roads.

"The next day, we started getting donations," Loyd recalls.

The result was a lighted baseball park with covered grandstand — "like a small major league park of that time" — and the Boston Braves did play an exhibition game in the new park the following year.

The park officially opened May 11, 1947, with *The Advocate* reporting that Shorty Loyd's mammoth homer provided garnish to a 5-4 conquest of Gonzales.

It wasn't the first ball to be hit out of the park, however, with a Gonzales player, Bill Midkiff, having that honor.

Loyd says an Indianapolis Triple-A team also did spring training in Victoria in 1947.

The park was built entirely with donated funds and labor, such as Central Power and Light Co. furnishing all the labor to put up the lights.

"Lots of people helped in the construction," Loyd recalls. "It was a community effort."

He is modest about his efforts, saying that "Victoria was so ripe and so ready for this that anybody could have done it."

Interest in baseball after the war had been generated when local players began scheduling games and the postwar Rosebuds were a result, with Loyd as the first manager.

"The old Guadalupe Valley League had been revived as a semipro league," he says, "and the Rosebuds went a step farther by playing semipro teams out of the area, as far away as Sinton, Conroe and Alpine."

Loyd managed the postwar semipro team through 1949 and served as business manager under Albert Alkek's sponsorship in 1950 when the team won the Houston Post Semi-Pro Championship, it being one of the major national tournaments of that time.

They had been the runners-up the year before.

A second baseman, Loyd says he had relinquished those duties to a younger player, Eddie Ganem, but continued to play utility and pinch hit until 1949.

The team disbanded after 1950 and the stadium was later refurbished by Tom O'Connor Jr. after he and his brother, Dennis O'Connor, purchased the professional team that had been brought to Victoria by Derrest

Williams in 1956 from Texas City. By the end of the season, the O'Connors had complete ownership and their Texas League Rosebuds continued to use the stadium through the 1960 season.

There had been many good amateur and semipro baseball players in Victoria, and Loyd thinks his late brother, Lynn, was "probably the best."

"Lynn could have gone on to professional ball," he says.

A first baseman and outfielder, Lynn Loyd had started playing in the service and joined the new Rosebuds after the war, but came down with polio in 1950.

"Billy Sherman was another outstanding player," Loyd recalls.

Baseball was a family thing with the Loyds, their father, R.E. Loyd, having played Class D professional ball for a year at Bonham before coming to Victoria to work for Southern Pacific around 1919 and to play ball for the railroad's semipro team.

By the time Shorty Loyd was five or six years old, he was accompanying his father to games all over Texas as the team's bat boy.

"They had a Pullman car just for the ball club," he says. "That was my first inkling what baseball was all about. I knew that ball players were treated as something special. That impressed me a whole lot and made me want to be a ball player."

He played in the '30s for the Junior Rosebuds, later with the prewar Rosebuds, in 1938 with the St. Louis Brown's farm club in Refugio, in 1941 with Heinie Baumgarten's semipro Gulf Oilers at Rosenburg, and with Army teams while in the service.

But, after the war, it was a new era for Shorty Loyd and baseball in Victoria when the community got together and built Riverside Stadium.

Kinda put Victoria on the map.

THE END